JOURNEY

Model

GOODNESS

Seeking Our Truth

Bestselling Author
ESTHER RENEE' WRIGHT, MSP, LCDC

Journey Model Goodness

Copyright© 2014 Esther Renee' Wright

ISBN# 13: 9780989201018
ISBN-10: 0989201015
LCCN: 2014917007

Cover Art by Tamika Hall | Tamikaink.com

Edited and Formatting by Tamika Hall

Marketing Branding Coach, Author Lá Tanyha Boyd known as Faith Abeliever- Founder of FAB Virtual Book Tours | Marketing Branding Coach | Social Media Strategist | Internet Book Publicist | 3x's Bestselling Author

Forward by Dr. Natalie E. Francisco

TESTIMONIALS

"Anyone involved in their own self-improvement journey will treasure this book because it provides another avenue to help Women become reflective, observant, introspective…the Models of Goodness they wish them to become."
~**Yolanda Carroll,** Abundant Love Christian Center, Houston, Texas

Journey Model Goodness is a devotional that has found a permanent place on my desk and heart. The daily reading of this book is great because it reminds me that God is working in each one of us. To be able to use the past as a stepping stone and lead us into our tomorrow of new beginnings. The results of this book can help to mend the broken pieces, alleviate fear and anxiety, and guide the reader to move forward in this journey we call life. In addition, the author helps to boost positive behavior, motivate, and lift your spirits to a place of peace within. I highly recommend Journey Model Goodness to everyone.
~**LáTanyha Boyd**, Empowerment Coach, 3x's Bestselling Author & International Radio Host of Spiritual Food for Thought Global Radio

What a way to jumpstart your daily meditation with this enlightening devotional written by "Renee", as I know her. Journey Model Goodness will cause you to reflect on your own personal journey in life to determine if the seeds you sow, the relationships you encounter and the words you speak model, "goodness." Renee's transparency and love for God can easily be seen through these devotionals, that will both encourage you and challenge you to live your life to the fullest!
~**Kendra Adams,** Author of, "Rescued by Love"

I would like to dedicate this book first to God and then in loving memory of my Father James E. Evans my aunt, Alice Ceasar and to all who are seeking their truth!!!

MODEL GOODNESS!!!

DEVOTIONAL INDEX

Foreword
Dr. Natalie A. Francisco
http://journey.nataliefrancisco.com

There are many who are looking for a way in to jumpstart their personal and professional lives with something that will stimulate their thinking and motivate them in their daily living. This latest book by my friend, Esther Renee Wright, is a timely and provocative resource that will accomplish all this and more for those who dare to delve into the pages of this 100-day journey toward modeling goodness that certainly leads to living a good quality life.

Renee, as I affectionately call her, has done a remarkable job of sharing personal reflections, practical anecdotes and sound wisdom that will guide readers in deciding and determining to discover the life that God our creator has in store for each of us. Life, within itself, is not just a process. It is a journey that is to be lived with meaning and that fuels our passion and purpose daily. This book provides us with a daily dose of energy and synergy to jumpstart our spirit, mind and body to work together to see and live life from a new perspective and paradigm, which in turn, attracts goodness to us in the form of thoughts, relationships, and blessings too numerous to name as we are transformed from the inside out with God's help and our own participation.

Thank you Renee for answering the clarion call to write this book, for in so doing, others will see and understand the value of their own life's journey and the abundant goodness that awaits them.

Welcome to JOURNEY MODEL GOODNESS, I
thank you in advance for including this little book
in a very important time of your day. I was inspired
to create this due to experiences I have had on my
journey. What the enemy meant for bad, God is and
will use for GOOD . . . I look forward to our
journey together! Journey

Model Goodness!

What is a journey? Using words from one of my
favorite authors, Melody Beattie, "a journey is trips
that will test your beliefs, remind you of old
lessons, and teach you some new ones. A journey is
able to breathe life with the potential to transform
that life into an adventure". . . Therefore take the
journey it is so worth the trip! Model Goodness!

Introduction

When I think of the word, "journey," a great deal of images come to mind: a path through trees, maybe grass and rocks, in some cases it may be a field of flowers, the image of cities I have never been, even meeting people I have never met. The word "journey," brings me to reflect on issues that don't "taste" good like ice cream, but ultimately bring about amazingly good like ice cream feelings.

When I look back over my life, I can honestly say I have been on a journey. Not all of it Modeled Goodness. I was asked one day what was one of my favorite memories and although I could come up with many, like sitting on my knees at the kitchen table as my Grandmother mixed the cake she made from scratch and waiting for the spoon or whatever she left in the bowl so I could lick what was left. Sometimes, I believe she would leave just a little bit in the bowl just for me. I could say the day I walked across the stage to receive my Bachelor's degree after many years of attempting to complete it. I tried to give up but God would not let me. I could have said my favorite memory was the day God blessed me to walk across the stage a second time to receive my Master's degree in Psychology, but what I said instead was the day after many years of dealing with my drug addiction,(and now being sober for 26 years), sitting in my room I was renting, one beautiful Saturday morning....I realized I could hear the BIRDS SINGING!!!

This may not mean anything to anyone, but if you had been where I had been, taken the journey I had taken all you would see was total darkness even in the daytime. There were no Birds singing in my life and if they were I could not hear them. What I could hear though was DEATH! God gave me another chance at getting it right...not perfect, but right.

Living life the best I can at my own level of excellence. Hoping that someone will be inspired and motivated by knowing if God did it for me, He will do it for you! Here I am over 25 years sober and still hearing the birds singing!

Take the journey and you too can hear the birds singing! I choose LIFE not DEATH! I want to Model Goodness rather than worthless movement!

In Titus Chapter 2:1-8, I love how the Message Bible states the mandate given to us: *"A God-Filled Life [1-6] Your job is to speak out on the things that make for solid doctrine. Guide older men into lives of temperance, dignity, and wisdom, into healthy faith, love, and endurance. Guide older women into lives of reverence so they end up as neither gossips nor drunks, but* <u>*models of goodness.*</u> *By looking at them, the younger women will know how to love their husbands and children, be virtuous and pure, keep a good house, be good wives. We don't want anyone looking down on God's Message because of their behavior. Also, guide the young men to live disciplined lives.[7-8] But mostly, show them all this by doing it yourself, incorruptible in your teaching, your words solid and sane.*

So, I ask you does this mean we have to be perfect? No, that is impossible, but what we can do is teach the lessons of our lives even in our imperfections. God wants us to be examples to those who are watching us so desperately seeking their way. I want so much to be that example for someone, anyone who may see me on my journey modeling goodness at my own level of excellence!

Here is an example of what my journey and maybe even yours can sometimes looks like: **JOURNEY ~ Check Your Motives!** Life is always pulling us in one direction or another, and in the pulling we all have to make decisions to do or not do. Before you, *do* what is your consideration for the DOING? I was recently asked to do something for someone and in my heart I felt my answer should be, "no," but I said "yes," for fear of not doing what looked like a Christian should do. WRONG ANSWER!

As I was about to get in motion to honor my, "YES", I said to myself, "You need to pray." So I asked God what would He have me to do, and He gave me direction. After doing what I heard in my spirit to do, I realized my motive for doing what I was about to do, was not about truly helping the individual. It was more about what I felt it would look like if I said, "no." Here is the vital part; my, "*yes*" was an answer that would have harmed the individual much more than my, "*no*." God asked me, "How will it be possible for the person to reach the state of change if you and so many others keep throwing a lifeline? You are helping that person to continue in the behavior."

WOW! So, I retracted my, "yes," and got out of the way so that God could do what was needed.

My challenge to you is check your motives, are you doing it for you or for what's best which always brings God's Glory! Karl Marx is quoted saying, *"Give a man a fish and you feed him for a day; teach a man to fish and you feed him for a lifetime."*

I love what the Message Bible says in Matthew 5:37 -*You don't make your words true by embellishing them with religious lace. In making your speech sound more religious, it becomes less true. Just say 'yes' and 'no.' When you manipulate words to get your own way, you go wrong.*

God Bless you and Model Goodness!

Esther Renee' Wright, MSP, LCDC

Day 1
JOURNEY~ HAPPY NEW DAY!!!

Well, it's a new day and there is excitement in the air! Now is the time to get our feet moving to allow the excitement to manifest itself into actual fruit from its presence. TIME TO MOVE, TIME TO DO, TIME TO BE ACCOUNTABLE, TIME TO EMBRACE, TIME TO LIVE WITH PASSION . . . The New Day is here and God is willing to walk through it with us! LET'S GO!

The Daily Word, January 1, 2014, blessed me with this: *CELEBRATE ~ I celebrate life! New beginnings are cause for celebration. Like the rising sun shining bright in the eastern sky, a fresh start is reason to rejoice. As we celebrate, we let go of the past and embrace the present. We discover a new opportunity to awaken to the power of the Holy Spirit within.*

Some celebrations are filled with cheers, songs, and shouts of encouragement; while others are quiet, like the blossoming of a flower. I celebrate life as a continuous learning experience, a gift of growth and expansion from a loving God. I acknowledge and revere life's varied celebrations. Joyous in the eternal power and love of God, I celebrate all of life.

I will cause your name to be celebrated in all generations; therefore the peoples will praise you forever and ever. Psalm 45:17

Modeling Goodness!

JOURNAL

Day 2
Journey ~ Sharing how you feel!

This question came across my mind, Why is it so hard for people to share how they feel? I am sure there are a lot of reasons that could be mentioned, but one reason I know of for sure is this – sometimes it's difficult to share because of how you feel after you say what it is you need to say. Everything inside of you says, "They don't understand, they think I am crazy, wow did that sound selfish, I did not use the right words, man, I should not have said anything."

The response or reactions of the individual we share with is so vital because it may determine whether you do it again. Sometimes, how we feel makes others feel as well, and because they have not chosen to feel an emotion, the response or reaction of their own feelings and not yours. We also have to understand that the enemy is counting on us to be silent. His mission is to kill, steal and destroy. . .so here is my challenge to you: **discover that individual you feel comfortable enough with who does not make you feel judged, stupid, crazy, discounted, tolerated.** That person who loves you in spite of and willing to help rather than run due to their own stuff. Maybe between the two of you, you both can be helped!!!

Modeling Goodness!

JOURNAL

_____
_____
_____
_____
_____
_____
_____
_____
_____
_____
_____
_____
_____
_____
_____
_____
_____
_____
_____
_____
_____
_____

Day 3
Journey ~ Shifting Into a Better Place!

When you hear the word, "shift," the first thing that comes to my mind is MOVE! But have we really thought about what that looks like? Well, if we did I believe one of the first things we would realize is, my shift won't look like your shift. So, it's necessary to seek the guidance of God to help understand what the *shift* is.

Shift what you ask? The answer is to shift from the unhealthy and that is not just about how we eat. So what does your unhealthy look like for YOU? We often talk about moving into what God has planned for us, but often we can't move because we don't know what it is we need to move away from. Shifting is not just a word we say, it has to have action behind it or it doesn't mean anything.

For many years I was so afraid to rely on what I felt in my heart. Feeling it would allow me to make the wrong decision. As a result I ultimately made the wrong choice. Because I followed the advice of my head rather than my heart, from where my passion and God lives. So, I am making the shift. . .the shift from my head to my heart. Will you shift with me? I believe it's God's will for my life.

Modeling Goodness!

JOURNAL

_____
_____
_____
_____
_____
_____
_____
_____
_____
_____
_____
_____
_____
_____
_____
_____
_____
_____
_____
_____

Day 4
Journey ~ A New Thing!

Often many of us wish we knew exactly how a situation was going to turn out. What will the outcome look like? Will I like it? will it be what I want? Will it change my life? We ask these questions seeking to see how this NEW THING God is about to do will fit into our lives. We really need to be careful with this, because in our quest to have what we want or think we want. We sometimes attempt to make things happen that were not meant to be, rather than waiting on God to do His NEW THING!

Wouldn't it be amazing if we had the capability to determine everything that was going to happen. I don't think so, knowing everything would stunt our growth and the word "experience" would no longer exist. What would we *MODEL* then? The JOURNEY would be pretty much non-existent, no surprises of events that could produce a smile, and the ups and downs that provides the wisdom of our lives which is an amazing tool to help others would be eliminated. The amazing aspects that allow our JOURNEY to breath and live.

Thank you God for, "You made me so happy, God I saw your work and I shouted for joy. How magnificent your work, God! How profound your **thought**s!" (Psalm 92:4, Msg.)

God's hand can always be trusted!

Modeling Goodness!

JOURNAL

_____
_____
_____
_____
_____
_____
_____
_____
_____
_____
_____
_____
_____
_____
_____
_____
_____
_____
_____
_____
_____
_____

Day 5
Journey ~ Do Your Words Edify or Hurt?

Today is another opportunity to either be of service to someone or tear someone down. I choose to be of service. How many times have we said something to someone and walked away trying to justify that what was said, needed to be said; however, in your heart of hearts you knew, you were wrong? I just hate when that happens. So when it does happen how do you fix it? Do you go back to the person and say what needs to be said or just continue to justify because you don't want to be wrong?

Well, the Bible says, in Ephesians 4:29 Amplified Bible (AMP): *Let no foul or polluting language, nor evil word nor unwholesome or worthless talk [ever] come out of your mouth, but only such [speech] as is good and beneficial to the spiritual progress of others, as is fitting to the need and the occasion, that it may be a blessing and give grace (God's favor) to those who hear it.*

Chew on that for a minute. . . OUCH!!!

Modeling Goodness!

JOURNAL

_____
_____
_____
_____
_____
_____
_____
_____
_____
_____
_____
_____
_____
_____
_____
_____
_____
_____
_____
_____
_____
_____
_____

Day 6
Journey ~ Forgive You Say?

This morning I discovered or had a sense that something was not just right in my spirit. I pretty much knew why and wondered what I was going to do. As always, God provides answers for me as well as I am sure He does for you. The answer was, "FORGIVE . . . not just those you feel have harmed you."

"Well, who do I need to forgive?" This is a good question and the answer is that we need to forgive ourselves. Why? Because out of that unforgiveness we make decisions consciously and many times unconsciously sabotage our moving forward.

Now why would we want to sabotage ourselves? Another good question, we do it because we don't feel worthy of the movement that could take place in our lives. So, what is it that you need to ask God to forgive you for, and then ask yourself to forgive you as well? Truth be told you are the only one holding you hostage, God has already forgiven you! His Word says in Psalm 103:12, *He has removed our sins as far from us as the east is from the west.* Now that is true forgiveness, we just need to give it to ourselves!

Modeling Goodness!

JOURNAL

Day 7
Journey ~ How Low Can You Go?

Have you ever met someone who has achieved what you would love to achieve in your life only to find yourself holding contempt in your heart for them? It seems that this individual, just knows everything – well, how low will you go? Will you go low enough to settle on your knees and pray for that individual and yourself? Or will you continue to do those things that God is certainly not pleased with, to prove to him or her that they are no better than you?

Perhaps that person is in our life to help propel us forward toward the achievement we have been too afraid to embark upon. Maybe that person is the mirror we need to look at, to work on some behavior we are exhibiting. Whatever the case may be, how low will you go? Prayer changes things, attitudes don't.

Modeling Goodness!

JOURNAL

_____
_____
_____
_____
_____
_____
_____
_____
_____
_____
_____
_____
_____
_____
_____
_____
_____
_____
_____
_____
_____
_____
_____

Day 8
Journey ~ Are You Growing?

As I sit here thinking about the growth process of nature, I wonder if we understand that the process nature goes through is really the same process humans go through. Before a seed is planted in dirt, the dirt has to be prepared for the process to be successful. In the preparation stage the dirt has to be tested. Tested for its strength and to see if it will need fertilizer or something to give the foundation the ability to produce healthy outcomes.

Does any of this sound familiar? I am not a gardener so I may not be able to express the complete process, but what I do know is, whenever God has a seed to plant in our lives, He prepares us for the growing process. The seed has to grow and for that to happen there is some preparation to be done for us to produce healthy outcomes. If you feel like you are being toiled and turned, and it doesn't quite feel or smell good, if the process is taking longer than you think, remember for a good healthy outcome, growing takes time. If we rush the process we might wither!

-Ruth 3:18 *Wait, my daughter, until you learn how the matter turns out.*

Modeling Goodness!

JOURNAL

_____
_____
_____
_____
_____
_____
_____
_____
_____
_____
_____
_____
_____
_____
_____
_____
_____
_____
_____
_____
_____
_____

Day 9
Journey ~ Are you waiting?

I guess you are wondering, what is she talking about today? Well, is there something you are waiting on? Are you waiting for things to get better before you take that step in the direction of where YOU know God is calling you? Are you waiting for the right time to make that call to say, I forgive you or that I am sorry to whomever you KNOW you need to say this too? Are you waiting until the right person comes along before you take that cruise or buy that house, or LIVE? As I watch my Father lie in ICU waiting for a heart to become available, it dawn on me AGAIN, that he is powerless on when the heart will become available. But you and I are not powerless in starting to do those things we have been waiting to do, for whatever reason. Life is amazing, and we should be living it as if that is true. We will never know when the day will come that we may be lying in ICU of life waiting...and can't don't anything about it.

Modeling Goodness!

JOURNAL

_____

_____

_____

_____

_____

_____

_____

_____

_____

_____

_____

_____

_____

_____

_____

_____

_____

_____

_____

_____

_____

_____

_____

Day 10
Journey ~ Don't Grow Weary!!!

As I have thought about the suicide of Robin Williams, I want to be even more transparent in hopes that someone will realize they are not alone. I truly understand what it feels like when life is overwhelming and as Robin Williams said in an interview, "That small voice in your head says, jump!"

I hear others saying, "There is nothing that bad that should make a person want to kill themselves." To those who feel that way, it may be true for them. I can tell you life sometimes happens and many have the thought of those feelings saying, "I CAN'T DO THIS!" I can't tell you how many times, that thought has showed up in my head. I really do wish I knew an antidote that could be given to an individual when the day comes that at even a fleeting thought of wanting to die could be given to wash it away. There may not be a physical pill or potion, but what I do know that works, is my ability to say, "God I need YOU!"

I realize there are many who may not feel they have a relationship with God, where this call to Him would be answered. But I wrote this to say, whether you have called on him once, 100 times or never He is *always* available to you. He is waiting on your call, so before you decide that life is too overwhelming, please call His name first and give Him a chance to answer. Trust me, I know what I know for myself! He will answer. Why? Because he loves you no matter what!

Modeling Goodness!

JOURNAL

_____
_____
_____
_____
_____
_____
_____
_____
_____
_____
_____
_____
_____
_____
_____
_____
_____
_____
_____
_____
_____
_____
_____

Day 11
Journey ~ Willing to Yield

What does the word, "yielding," really mean? When I think of this word I see a bright yellow triangle with the word YIELD written across it, but beyond that it means a great deal more. Yielding says, "I am willing to submit." It is a verbal act of renouncing a claim or right or position. It is a position that says, "I am inclined to yield to argument, influence or control."

The tension felt when frustrated should dissipate when we truly yield, because internally yielding is the lacking of stiffness and giving way to pressure then we are able to make or at least become willing to make concessions.

Why would we do these things? What benefit would yielding have in our lives? Well, if we are yielding and not just attempting to shut someone up, there can be peace. Does that five-letter word mean anything to you? Yielding brings about many benefits:

- Knowledge- yielding presents an opportunity to grasp something we never would have.
- Confidence- yielding does not mean we are weak, and just gave up, no, to the contrary, it takes strength to yield. Yielding says, "I am an agent of peace." James 3:17 says, *The wisdom from above is first pure, then peaceable, gentle, willing to yield, full of mercy and good fruits, without a trace of partiality.*

Modeling Goodness!

ESTHER RENEE' WRIGHT

JOURNAL

_____
_____
_____
_____
_____
_____
_____
_____
_____
_____
_____
_____
_____
_____
_____
_____
_____
_____
_____
_____
_____
_____
_____

Day 12
Journey ~ ACTION!

When I typed the word, "action," I saw the story in the Bible where talents were given to three different people. In Matthew 25:15 it says, *And unto one he gave five talents, to another two, and to another one; to every man according to his several ability; and straightway took his journey.* Each person did something different with what they were given, and according to the *action* they took determined the outcome they were blessed with.

What talents have you been given? Has God given you something to do and you buried it for a rainy day? What if that rainy day never comes? What blessing has been received from what He has given you? What if what you buried had my blessing attached to it?

It is time to take action in our lives and do what needs to be done. This is not just for ourselves because our received blessings usually have a trickledown effect. It is time to take action!

Modeling Goodness!

JOURNAL

Day 13
Journey ~ Peace!

As I sit here with my best friend, Mr. Titus, my dog, I realize that we sometimes make life a lot harder than it needs to be. Mr. Titus is in a position where he has to totally rely on me for him to eat, to have a roof over his head, to go outside, to have his toys he plays with. Mr. Titus' life depends on me to provide the things he needs to live. When I put myself in the same position as Mr. Titus, my life depends on God to provide the things I need to live. Yes, I go to a job that pays me a salary, but who provided the job? GOD! I know I get in my car everyday to drive where I need to be, and who provided the car? GOD! I have food in my refrigerator that is so needed for the nourishment of my body, who provided the food? GOD!

These are just a few things God provides for me, don't let me start talking about the activity of my limbs and how I can see, hear, talk and be of a sound mind! I think you get it. ENOUGH SAID! PEACE!

Romans 15:13 *May the God of hope fill you with all joy and peace as you trust in him, so that you may overflow with hope by the power of the Holy Spirit.*

1 Thessalonians 5:23 *May God himself, the God of peace, sanctify you through and through.* May your whole spirit, soul and body be kept blameless at the coming of our Lord Jesus Christ.

Modeling Goodness!

JOURNAL

_____
_____
_____
_____
_____
_____
_____
_____
_____
_____
_____
_____
_____
_____
_____
_____
_____
_____
_____
_____
_____
_____

Day 14
Journey ~ Protect you!

It can be really difficult to protect yourself from the words, actions, and judgments of others. We have to remember that hurt people *hurt* people. Is that on purpose? Maybe, maybe not, but how do we stand against the pains and misery that may be projected on us? I believe we protect ourselves by not doing what we believe others may have done or is doing to us. If someone has lied to you, YOU tell the truth! If someone has said hurt words to you, YOU speak kindness as often as you can! If someone has deceived you, YOU let your YES BE YES!

How do I allow ME to be that which I wish I saw in others? Good question, God who is a God who can't lie, and not only can He not lie He just won't, says, in His Word that He answers with Yes and Amen. So because we are a people who can lie and we all know we will, living by the power of God who lives inside each of us, His power to answer, "Yes and Amen," gives us the power to allow our YES to be YES!

Be the person you desire others to be in your life, and you will always walk away saying if nothing else, "There are two things I can learn what I want to be like and what I don't. My YES IS YES and I am pretty proud of that!

Modeling Goodness!

JOURNAL

_____
_____
_____
_____
_____
_____
_____
_____
_____
_____
_____
_____
_____
_____
_____
_____
_____
_____
_____
_____
_____
_____
_____

Day 15
Journey ~ Our Diamonds!

How do you perceive your experiences? Do you see them as a hardship or diamonds in your toolbox? I recently learned a new set of words to use rather than, "toolbox." It was said that we all have different backpacks. In your own personal backpack, are you being weighed down by the heaviness of your God-allowed experiences or are you carrying around some valuable information?

I can truly say that God created each of us for a purpose, and the direction in how we get to that purpose may not be the path we would choose for ourselves. But what I know for sure is even though I would have attempted to change the experiences I have had, God's direction has been amazing! Our experiences are truly diamonds and they are diamonds not for us, but for others who come along our path. So, please allow yourself to find the SHINE in your backpack, dullness does not look good on you! SHINE ON WITH YOUR SHINING SELF!!!

Modeling *Goodness!*

JOURNAL

_____
_____
_____
_____
_____
_____
_____
_____
_____
_____
_____
_____
_____
_____
_____
_____
_____
_____
_____
_____
_____
_____
_____

Day 16
Journey ~ How Important Are YOU?

There are many times when we are so busy making sure everyone is okay, that we forget about ourselves. How many times have we heard this? How many times has someone share powerful life changing encouragement with us and at the time it touched our hearts, but we walked away taking care of everything and everybody but *us*. Proverbs 11:14 says, *For lack of guidance a nation falls, but victory is won through many advisers.* That guidance can also come through the most important person in our lives, and this YOU!

I say that because we have to give ourselves permission to accept the guidance and accept the adviser's advice. If you feel like something is missing in your life, or you find yourself saying, "Why don't I feel like I am moving?" Then it is time to give yourself some amazing advice. Say to yourself, "GIRL OR MAN IT IS TIME TO ALLOW THE GUIDANCE GOD HAS PLACED BEFORE ME, TO KEEP YOU FROM FALLING AND ALLOW VICTORY TO BE WON THROUGH THE ADVICE!!

Modeling Goodness!

JOURNAL

_____
_____
_____
_____
_____
_____
_____
_____
_____
_____
_____
_____
_____
_____
_____
_____
_____
_____
_____
_____
_____
_____

Day 17
Journey ~ I know I am being LED and so are you!

Do you have certain things you think about often and wonder what you are suppose to do with them? Or, are you wondering if those things will ever change? Even when is does not feel like it, God is guiding us. We are being led. There are times when life flows along and when it's easy and natural to believe we're being guided. Then there comes a point in any journey, in even the most magical of trips, when we look around and say, "I don't know where I'm going."

We don't have a plan, we're short on ideas, and we're plumb out of vision. We've seen as far as we can see. Now is the time to practice what we know: TRUST, LET GO, and STAY AS PEACEFUL as we can. Stay right here in the present moment and let the journey unfold. Trust that you are being guided and led. God said He would never leave us, nor forsake us, and we're standing on his Word!

Modeling Goodness!

JOURNAL

_____
_____
_____
_____
_____
_____
_____
_____
_____
_____
_____
_____
_____
_____
_____
_____
_____
_____
_____
_____
_____
_____
_____

Day 18
Journey ~ YOUR WORD!

Isaiah 55:11 says, *So is my word that goes out from my mouth: It will not return to me empty, but will accomplish what I desire and achieve the purpose for which I sent it.* God is saying that His word has power, it is truth, it is dependable. We can count on what He says because He will not say anything over our lives that is not true!

I could run right here! Knowing that we serve a God who wants us to know that we can trust what he says, just makes my heart dance. Then I looked at my word – your word that says, can those in my/your life trust what you or I say? Or do they walk away saying, "I'll believe it when I see it!"

When someone needs to share something at a very critical and confidential moment in their lives, can they call you? I don't know about you but I want my word to be just as powerful as the God who lives inside me. I want to be trusted and dependable, what about you?

Modeling Goodness!

JOURNAL

_____

_____

_____

_____

_____

_____

_____

_____

_____

_____

_____

_____

_____

_____

_____

_____

_____

_____

_____

_____

_____

_____

Day 19
Journey ~ What do you stand for?

I was asked if I had someone who inspired me to pursue some of the things in my life. My response was Nelson Mandela, because he was a man who stood beyond himself for what he truly believed in, and because he stood, there was some major accomplishments achieved. I also mentioned Martin Luther King, Jr. because he also stood pass himself, for the rights of humanity. What impressed me most about that was the fact that his standing was not about one race, he stood for people whomever his standing would make life better for them. My third person was my Co-pastor Mia Wright; she inspires me through her leadership in ministry and her heart for the betterment of people. God has blessed her to lead what was once a women's service that met one time a month, into what is known now as an International Ministry, touching the lives of many people. It is my desire to stand and not just stand, but be an ambassador of change, for the people of this world! I AM STANDING! What about you?

Modeling Goodness!

JOURNAL

_____
_____
_____
_____
_____
_____
_____
_____
_____
_____
_____
_____
_____
_____
_____
_____
_____
_____
_____
_____
_____

Day 20
Journey ~ Pay attention to what you SEE!!!

I have been quiet lately, not on purpose but just trying to keep up with the changes in my life. Wrapping my mind around the reality of the events that have taken place and are going on right now. In my meditation time something was brought back to me. I remember having a conversation with a friend one day, and at that time everything was going good in my life. In this conversation, she said something like, "You need to enjoy the good while it is happening because just like the good came, it could go."

I didn't realize this at the time, but I believe that due to a lot of bad, or things just not seeming to go as I would have liked them to go in my past. I think I focused more on the last part of her statement. I look back now and realize I had been waiting for the good to go rather than enjoying it truly to the utmost. Cheating myself of the full experience of the blessings taking place. So be careful how you take in the words of others, not that her words were bad or wrong, I just needed to change my view!

How you do life is in your PERCEPTION. WHAT DO YOU SEE?

Modeling Goodness!

JOURNAL

_____
_____
_____
_____
_____
_____
_____
_____
_____
_____
_____
_____
_____
_____
_____
_____
_____
_____
_____

Day 21
Journey ~ What Have you Paid Forward?

I have not been able to post like I so enjoy, my computer works when it wants to recently. But I thought I should take the opportunity to post this since my laptop decided to participate. I have to say that I ABSOLUTELY LOVE FACEBOOK!!! As a lot of you know - but let me tell you why. I recently posted that my parents Mr. and Mrs. James Evans were celebrating 50 years of marriage; which I so wish I would have been able to do. Some wonderful person read that post, found my Dad who, for those of you who may not know, is in ICU, called him and said: "I don't know you, and you don't know me, but I saw it posted on Facebook that you and your wife were celebrating 50 years of marriage, and I just thought that was awesome. I wanted to say to you, may God bless you and make you whole.

I want to say, "thank you," to whoever was kind enough to PAY IT FORWARD by considering my Dad.

Numbers 6:25 (TLB) 24-26 *May the Lord bless and protect you; may the Lord's face radiate with joy because of you; may he be gracious to you, show you his favor, and give you his peace.*

AWWWW. . . PRICELESS

Modeling Goodness!

JOURNAL

_____
_____
_____
_____
_____
_____
_____
_____
_____
_____
_____
_____
_____
_____
_____
_____
_____
_____
_____
_____
_____

Day 22
Journey ~ How Do You Affect Others?

For years I have attempted to be what I believe others wanted me to be, just to fit in. I found myself trying to downsize me to make others who were intimidated by me to make them feel better. I didn't realize what I was doing, because I didn't think highly enough of myself to think or believe that anyone would be intimidated by me. I remember a person saying to one day, "she did not like me" and I asked her why, what did I ever do to you? She responded with these words, "It's the God in you that I don't like."

I was shocked, but when I think about it, there are people who may not understand what it is about you they don't like. They don't understand what to do with what they believe they see in you that makes them uncomfortable. Could it be the God in YOU, the light that comes from you? Well, if that is a reason for someone to not like you, keep shining and keep being the light. It is our prayer that eventually that same light will bless their lives!!!

The Bibles says it like this in Matthew 5:10-17-*"10 Blessed are those who are persecuted because of righteousness, for theirs is the kingdom of heaven. 11 "Blessed are you when people insult you, persecute you and falsely say all kinds of evil against you because of me. 12 Rejoice and be glad, because great is your reward in heaven, for in the same way they persecuted the prophets who were before you.*

Salt and Light
13 "You are the salt of the earth. But if the salt loses its saltiness, how can it be made salty again? It is no longer good for anything, except to be thrown out and trampled underfoot. 14 "You are the light of the world. A town built on a hill cannot be hidden. 15 Neither do people light a

lamp and put it under a bowl. Instead they put it on its stand, and it gives light to everyone in the house. 16 In the same way, let your light shine before others, that they may see your good deeds and glorify your Father in Heaven.
AMEN AND PRAISE GOD FROM WHOM ALL BLESSINGS FLOW!!!

Modeling Goodness!

_____
_____
_____
_____
_____
_____
_____
_____
_____
_____
_____
_____
_____
_____
_____
_____
_____
_____
_____
_____
_____

Day 23
Journey ~ Everything is exactly the way it is suppose to be!

Do you believe that? Well, I find myself saying at times, "Things are exactly as they are suppose to be otherwise they would be different." Since we often quote the scripture Jeremiah 29:11, *For I know the plans I have for you," declares the Lord, "plans to prosper you and not to harm you, plans to give you hope and a future." I really like the way The King James version says it, "For I know the thoughts that I think toward you, saith the Lord, thoughts of peace, and not of evil, to give you an expected end.*

Either version speaks to the unknown that only God knows how the expected end looks. If that is true and since the Word of God is the truth in my life and I pray it is for you as well, then how can we doubt the events that are taking place in our lives? We doubt some things because those events do not look as we would have them. Those situations don't allow us to feel as we would have us to feel. What I know for sure is that God knows the thoughts that he thinks toward you and I. His thoughts have proven in my life that he uses what I would choose to remove as a blessing for someone else. Isn't it an amazing gift to be used by God? I say, "YES TO HIS WILL!"

Modeling Goodness!

JOURNAL

Day 24
Journey ~ Finding PEACE in the Midst of Calamity!

In this world today there are so many things going on that the words, "Finding peace," almost sounds like finding Nemo. In spite of all that Nemo goes through in his life, HE SURVIVES! I believe that if we could just remember that in spite of all the things we have gone through WE SURVIVED, and because of that remembrance, we could find PEACE in the midst of the present calamity. Does this mean we will be running around jumping for joy, maybe not. But it could mean I can get up put one foot in front of the other and TAKE THE DAY ON! Remember what it says in John 14:27 *"Peace I leave with you, My peace I give to you; not as the world gives do I give to you. Let not your heart be troubled, neither let it be afraid."*

Modeling Goodness!

JOURNAL

_____

_____

_____

_____

_____

_____

_____

_____

_____

_____

_____

_____

_____

_____

_____

_____

_____

_____

_____

_____

_____

_____

_____

Day 25
Journey ~ The start of a new work week, a new opportunity at life, a new way of seeing, doing, practicing, trusting, loving, forgiving, and a host of things NEW.

Sometimes doing something new brings about stress, being nervous, unwillingness, and sometimes complaints. When we operate in the negative instead of moving forward we digress in our movement, delaying the blessing of acceptance and peace. New does not always feel good like it would for me if I just got a new pair of shoes. But because character is being built in the NEW, the pain of doing it different from what was the norm, is like trying to swim against the current. So, what should we do? Relax, take a deep breath and go with the flow, saying to ourselves, God your will be done not mine! In Isaiah 43:19 scripture gives this amazing promise: "Behold, I will do a new thing, now it shall spring forth; Shall you not know it? I will even make a road in the wilderness and rivers in the desert." Don't let your fear of the NEW make you miss the blessing of SPRINGING FORWARD!

Modeling Goodness!

JOURNAL

Day 26
Journey ~ All is in Divine ORDER!

My mind is racing this morning with a lot of thoughts, feelings, and for some reason a sense of urgency. I am not sure what the urgency is about but what I do know is no matter what, ALL IS IN DIVINE ORDER! There are events that have taken place in our lives that make us feel there is a need DO SOMETHING. Sometimes we need to stop, relax, pray, and wait for God to answer. It is in the DOING SOMETHING that we sometimes DO TOO MUCH, or NOT DO ENOUGH! Either way, in realizing that ALL IS IN DIVINE ORDER we have the opportunity to be lead and be at peace.

The light of God surrounds me, the love of God enfolds me. The Power of God protects me, the presence of God watches over me. WHEREVER I AM, GOD IS AND ALL IS IN DIVINE ORDER! Now take a deep breath and feel the peace? ALL IS IN DIVINE ORDER!

Modeling Goodness!

JOURNAL

Day 27
Journey ~ MY LIGHT!

It is truly my desire that my light within me shines so bright that when others encounter it, they know and see God! Does shining mean, I will be laughing and beaming over with joy? Does it mean I will have this appearance of peace over me that it looks like I am floating? No, the truth is some days, we may not feel that our lights are shining, but what I know for sure is the light NEVER goes out! Whether I am gleaming with joy or a little down from some circumstance, my LIGHT our LIGHTS NEVER goes out! Why? Because God is always with us, in every experience we walk through.

I choose to walk through my life with realness so that others can see that dealing with life is not going to always be happy go lucky. But life can and will be dealt with through the Power of our Loving GOD! He is GREATER than anything that may come our way! So when life feels heavy always remember you are not carrying it alone. There is an important reason for the experience, learn the lesson and SHINE AS YOU WALK WITH GOD THROUGH IT!

Luke 11:33 - *No one after lighting a lamp puts it in a cellar, but on the lamp stand so that those who enter may see the light!*

YOU ARE SHINING RIGHT NOW!

Modeling Goodness!

JOURNAL

Day 28

Journey ~ Be Strong and Courageous!

As Joshua was given the task of taking over when Moses died to lead the people of God into the promise land. (Joshua 1: 1-9) God told him some very important facts, which I believe should we apply those same facts to our lives we would be successful wherever we go. So my question to you this morning is, how are you viewing your promise land? Are you feeling some fear about what you see? Are you wondering if you can do it? Are you concerned if you fit in or not? If so I came today to say, "Don't be scared because God is with you wherever you go!"

Listen, do you want to be a success? Of course you do! Everybody does. God told Joshua, and He tells us, how to be successful in our lives advancing the Kingdom of God and receiving an abundant life...

1. Be Strong
2. Be Courageous, letting the small irritants of life build your character
3. Be Obedient to God's Word
4. Be Dependent on God in the Big Issues of Life

Modeling Goodness!

JOURNAL

_____
_____
_____
_____
_____
_____
_____
_____
_____
_____
_____
_____
_____
_____
_____
_____
_____
_____
_____
_____
_____

Day 29
Journey ~ It's the Holiday Season!

As we embark upon the holiday season which can be anytime of the year. Not just November and December. We need to be aware that some of us are overjoyed by the upcoming weeks. Then there are some of us who experience a difficult time. For those who love the holidays and are sooooo looking forward to it. Be aware of your friends and family who may be struggling. Don't ignore it, they won't say anything, but they will need you!

God showed me these rules through Joshua 1:1-9 a couple things we need to remember when faced with events in our lives that may be challenging. I will share these with you this week. He gave Joshua four rules for him to be successful and they apply to us today.

The first rule is: Be Strong. If we are going to be successful with dealing with the issues of our lives and not operate out of our fears, we first of all have to be strong. The word "strong" in this context, means "to fasten upon" attach to something that can help you remain anchored. Not just anchored but anchored in what will help you stand in what you know to be true.

Joshua 1:9 *Have I not commanded you? Be strong and courageous. Do not be terrified; do not be discouraged, for the LORD your God will be with you wherever you go.*

Modeling Goodness!

JOURNAL

Day 30
Journey ~ What a Difference a Day Makes!

I say out loud and boldly, "I LOVE GOD!" There is no hesitation, no put my head down when I say it. I say it with conviction and admiration! Psalm 147:5 says, *Great is our Lord, and of great power. His understanding is infinite.* Yesterday started as an emotional day for me. I prayed and asked God to help me to the other side of the lessons I am in the midst of learning. Because of his power and greatness He blessed me with several revelations to the lessons all in one day.

- Lesson 1: WE NEED PEOPLE. He placed two amazing people before me to help me gain strength when I needed it most. We never have to walk alone.
- Lesson 2: Get out of self and be of service. He placed a person in front of me, who needed my help. When you are helping others you don't have time to be in self!
- Lesson 3: When you think God does not understand. HE DOES! When I got home someone in another state was thinking enough of me to send me an amazing, "just because" gift. So, when you say God knows your heart, He really does and He always, let me say that again ALWAYS provides what we need. I needed love and compassion and HE DELIVERED! At the end of the day I watched a video of a friend dancing to this new song named, "Happy!" This morning my radio came on with the same song playing!!! Wow, great is our lord, and of great power. His understanding is infinite."

Thank you God for loving and understanding me! Now it's your turn to allow God do for you what you can't do for yourself!

Modeling Goodness!

JOURNAL

Day 31
Journey ~ Oooooh the Holidays!

Let me first say, I apologize for the length today. But this is what God gave me! Have you realized that next week is Thanksgiving? Wow, it appears that time is moving so fast, and because of that we should not take this time for granted. It is my prayer that, no matter how you may feel about this time of the year, you will allow yourself to not be controlled by circumstances in our lives. That we allow ourselves to enjoy every second of what could and is for so many a joyous occasion.

We have been considering what God said to Joshua when he took over leading the people of Israel after Moses died. Major task don't you think? Well, we can sometimes feel just as Joshua probably felt when having to do something he did not feel he could do. So the third point on how we can be successful in dealing with this holiday season or areas of our lives that may appear larger than we believe we can bear is:

- **Be Obedient to His Word** - When we are told to be careful to obey, God is telling us, we can't pick and choose when we apply His Word to our lives. We must be consistently careful, as we come to understand God's Word, to consistently look for ways to apply it, and not violate it.
- Be alert to how the word of God applies to your life. Look for ways to apply it. Like Joshua we can only claim victory through obedience. Obedience takes strength and courage. Obedience takes a specific strength and courage that only comes through faith in God.

Joshua 1:7-8- *Be strong and very courageous. Be careful to obey all the law my servant Moses gave you; do not turn from it to the right or to the left, that you may be successful wherever you go. 8 Do not let this Book of the Law depart from your mouth; meditate on it day and night, so that you may be careful to do everything written in it. Then you will be prosperous and successful.*

Modeling Goodness!

Day 32
Journey ~ Listen to Your HEART

God speaks there! Do you realize that the guidance of God is an energy that is moving, pushing, pulling, and guiding us forward each moment of the day? God is so busy in each moment leading us towards our destiny. Let God guide you forward. Let Him move you along. Listen to your heart. It will take you; move you to where you need to go. I wish I could say you will be able to see as far ahead as you would like. But if we were able to, that ability would prevent us from listening, trusting, opening to the amazing guidance that comes from God.

So, how do we listen to our hearts? Stay in the present? Be mindful of what is going on around you. Listen to that small still voice, speaking from your heart. Trust the wisdom that God has given you, the wisdom that will guide you and move you to where God is leading you. Our Destiny is there to be embraced, and we are in partnership with God in creating it by the choices we make each step of the way! God Speaks through your heart; so let your choices come from there!

Modeling Goodness!

JOURNAL

_____
_____
_____
_____
_____
_____
_____
_____
_____
_____
_____
_____
_____
_____
_____
_____
_____
_____
_____
_____
_____

Day 33
Journey ~ I know I am being LED and so are you!

Do you have certain things you think about often and wonder what you are suppose to do with them? Or are you wondering if those things will ever change? Even when it does not feel like it, God is guiding us. We are being led. There are times when life flows along and when it's easy and natural to believe we're being guided, but there comes a point in any journey, in even the most magical of trips, when we look around and say, "I don't know where I'm going."

We don't have a plan, we're short on ideas, and we're plumb out of vision. We've gone as far as we could see. Now is the time to practice what we know: TRUST, LET GO, STAY AS PEACEFUL as we can. Stay right here in the present moment and let the journey unfold. Trust that you are being guided and led! God said that He would never leave us, nor forsake us, and we're standing on his Word!

Modeling Goodness!

JOURNAL

_____

_____

_____

_____

_____

_____

_____

_____

_____

_____

_____

_____

_____

_____

_____

_____

_____

_____

_____

_____

_____

_____

Day 34
Journey ~ Are You Sure? Good question, are we ever sure about the decisions me make?

Are we ever sure about the people we depend on? Are we ever sure of the direction we should go? There are so many things that we count on every day, many things that we don't give a second thought to. We are so assured of many things in our lives and when the mess hits the fan, we then find ourselves asking the question, "How did I miss that?"

We missed it because we placed someone or something in the place of the only one we can totally depend on and that is God. People will fail us, not necessarily on purpose but being human we all make mistakes. The answer to our assurance in through prayer God leads and protects. This is what makes our trust and assurance real! Have you asked God to lead you in all areas of your life? It's not too late, start today!

Isaiah 32:17&18 *And the work of righteousness shall be peace; and the effect of righteousness quietness and assurance forever. 18 And my people shall dwell in a peaceable habitation, and in sure dwellings, and in quiet resting places*

BLESSED ASSURANCE!

Modeling Goodness!

JOURNAL

_____

_____

_____

_____

_____

_____

_____

_____

_____

_____

_____

_____

_____

_____

_____

_____

_____

_____

_____

_____

_____

_____

Day 35
Journey ~ What's Happening?

There's never a time when nothing is happening. Something is always taking place. Growth is occurring. We're evolving, transforming, working things out, incorporating our last lesson, preparing for our next. Something is happening. We just don't always see it, and that's how it's meant to be. When we see, when we know too much too soon, it's easy to let our heads get in the way. In these times we think we have to control, force, and make it happen, have to do something. In a gentle but wise way, God takes into account our fears and our natures. He doesn't let us know too much too soon. God doesn't spoil the surprise. He doesn't want us to spoil it either. So what we truly need to do is open our hearts to the power of God. Trust that something is always happening. And often, it's much different and better than you think.

God is so amazing and please remember what it says in *Isaiah 55:8 "For My thoughts are not your thoughts, Nor are your ways My ways," says the Lord.*

Modeling Goodness!

JOURNAL

_____
_____
_____
_____
_____
_____
_____
_____
_____
_____
_____
_____
_____
_____
_____
_____
_____
_____
_____
_____

Day 36
Journey ~ Moving Forward!

Each of us has experiences that give two types of mindsets: one is an attempt to forget those things that hurt us, and the other is to feel joy when reminded of a particular event or situation. Well, I believe that both have the ability to impact our lives in a positive way, if we allow it. That which we desire to forget is full of lessons that we need to move forward and accomplish the new blessings in our lives. Without those lessons we may visit those same events or situations in our future. The pains of our lives do not exist to simply make our hearts and souls hurt, they exist because there is purpose behind each one. Purpose we may not be aware of at the moment, but in trying to forget those things keeps us from ever seeing what the purpose was.

I am not suggesting that we dwell on the past, what I am suggesting is that we learn from the past. And allow it to propel us to a better future rather then keeping us hostage in something we cannot change. Then we may be able to feel more joy in our lives than we ever have before!

Philippians 3:12-16 The Message (MSG): 12-14 *I'm not saying that I have this all together, that I have it made. But I am well on my way, reaching out for Christ, who has so wondrously reached out for me. Friends, don't get me wrong: By no means do I count myself an expert in all of this, but I've got my eye on the goal, where God is beckoning us onward—to Jesus. I'm off and running, and I'm not turning back.* 15-16 *So let's keep focused on that goal, those of us who want everything God has for us. If any of you have something else in mind, something less than total commitment, God will clear your blurred vision— you'll see it yet! Now that we're on the right track, let's stay on it.*

Modeling Goodness!

JOURNAL

_____
_____
_____
_____
_____
_____
_____
_____
_____
_____
_____
_____
_____
_____
_____
_____
_____
_____
_____
_____

Day 37
Journey ~ Liar!!!

Last night I wrote a gratitude post on my personal page, and after writing I realized I could have written so much more for the blessings in my life are so many. Then this morning it only took one thing to attempt to change my gratitude to sadness. Well, I came by this morning to say, THE DEVIL IS A LIE AND THE TRUTH AINT IN HIM!!

So, as my friend said in this morning's prayer, "God when your presence seems far away, give us a gentle nudge to let us know you are there."

The enemy wants us to buy into those areas of our life that can make us feel sad, but, we know and BELIEVE in God's power to use those same areas to bless wherever He wants. Today when things attempt to crop up and irritate our spirit this is the day of holding our fist in the air and proclaiming, "THE DEVIL IS A LIE AND THE TRUTH AINT IN HIM!!!"

Let's go children of God, we have the power!

Modeling Goodness!

ESTHER RENEE' WRIGHT

JOURNAL

_____

_____

_____

_____

_____

_____

_____

_____

_____

_____

_____

_____

_____

_____

_____

_____

_____

_____

_____

_____

Day 38
Journey ~ Have you looked at YOU lately?

It is really easy to see the faults, blemishes and shortcomings of others. But what have you seen in yourself? Is there something in you that even you in the silence of your soul says. . .I really need to do something about that!!! I read a prayer written by Dr. Natalie Francisco from her book, "I'm Just Saying" and it speaks to this very issue:

"Father, search my mind and heart today and remove anything that is contrary to producing growth in my personal and professional life. I pray for discernment to see my own shortcomings rather than those of others, courage to acknowledge weak areas and wisdom to correct what is wrong while building upon the foundation of what is right. I thank you for allowing my actions to agree with my words as I evaluate myself and strive for excellence. In Jesus' Name. Amen."

Are you being your best YOU today? That option is available to us at any time we choose it!

Modeling Goodness!

JOURNAL

_____

_____

_____

_____

_____

_____

_____

_____

_____

_____

_____

_____

_____

_____

_____

_____

_____

_____

_____

_____

_____

_____

_____

Day 39
Journey ~ Who Do You Serve?

When I think of the word, "serve," I instantly envision a tray with items on it being placed in front of an individual to obtain whatever items they desire or need. Well, this is exactly what we are to do when we serve others, whether it be something tangible or intangible. Sometimes, we serve others thinking that what we have to give to them is exactly what they should want or need. The truth is that serving is not about us individually and whether the person or persons we are attempting to serve accepts what we have to offer or not, is really not the issue. The issue is we serve and God gives purpose and outcome to our service. We do the footwork and leave the rest to God! When we extend ourselves to others, we are saying, "God I am your vessel use me as you see fit."

For the responsibility of the outcome belongs to God. Serve, walk away praying that God's Will be done! Lord, your servant is listening!!

Truly I tell you, just as you did it to one of the least of these brothers and sisters of mine, you did for me -Matthew 25:40

Modeling Goodness!

JOURNAL

Day 40
Journey ~ I Matter!

Do you sometimes feel like you don't matter and that no one notices you? Maybe you don't feel that on a consistent basis, but the thought of, "Do I matter?" has come up. When I was a little girl, I remember asking God, "Why did you create me?"

I know I don't remember getting an answer, but I have some awesome realizations that gives me an answer today! I really do believe that if God had laid out his reasons for my existence, I wouldn't have believed it anyway. So He waited to show me rather than tell me. What has He shown you? I know for sure He has shown you that YOU MATTER!

So, do you matter? Yes, YOU do through your love you have healed many who have showed up on your *JOURNEY* and you will do the same today! Someone NEEDS YOUR LOVE!

Modeling Goodness!

JOURNAL

_____

_____

_____

_____

_____

_____

_____

_____

_____

_____

_____

_____

_____

_____

_____

_____

_____

_____

_____

_____

_____

Day 41
Journey ~ I'm a lighthouse shining for the whole world to see!

Have you found yourself asking, "Why am I going through this? I cannot see why this is a necessary event in my life." Many times things take place in our lives and at the time we don't understand it or see how it will benefit us. But when I look back, I truly do see the amazing lessons I learned. Well, a perspective change is what is needed. The things we face are preparation for the plan God has for our lives. There are some experiences we just have to have! Plan for these moments. They are not the end of the *JOURNEY*, they are the passageway through the tunnel and into the light. Soon, it will become clear we always come out of the darkness INTO THE MARVELOUS LIGHT!

Isaiah 58:8 *Then your light will break forth like the dawn, and your healing will quickly appear; then your righteousness will go before you, and the glory of the Lord will be your rear guard.*

So, keep it moving because Your Light WILL BREAK THROUGH! Your life will be a testimony to many! Remember, YOU'RE A LIGHTHOUSE SHINING FOR THE WHOLE WORLD TO SEE!

Modeling Goodness!

JOURNAL

Day 42
Journey ~ Answered Prayer!

There are so many times when prayers have been prayed and the results that took place may not have looked as what was being hoped for. As a result of that sometimes when we pray we may be praying with a little hesitation, why? Well it could be because we know what we would like to see happen, but yet is that desire the same as the plan of God? I had been recently praying for my Father that he be blessed to meet the criteria of being placed on the heart transplant list to save his life. I don't think I have to tell you what my desire was, but I must admit that it crossed my mind during the process of waiting for God to answer, "does my desire line up with God's Will?" Does that mean I doubt that God could do it? No, I knew that he could. I just needed to trust that whether His answer matched my desire or not, His plan is always BEST! Well, his plan matched my desire and my Father's name is now on the heart transplant list. Thank You God for showing part of your plan for his life!

We have to trust God even when his answer is not what we expected or desired!

Modeling Goodness!

JOURNAL

Day 43
Journey ~ Violence Is Never The Answer!

As I watch CNN last night reporting on the Ferguson grand jury decision, I was truly sadden. Sadden by two things, the disappointment of the people, and the reaction to the disappointment. I heard myself ask the question, "what is burning down that building going to change about the grand jury's decision?" Now more families are hurt, loss jobs, loss business of the owners who had nothing to do with the decision. People were physically hurt, and arrested. How did that help? Anger is a God given emotion, therefore, we are expected to become angry in life. But it is how and what we do with the anger that makes the difference. If responded to incorrectly, decisions are made that do more harm than good. In times like these, faith has to be at the core of our being. It may appear one way today, but God has the power to move mountains. IF WE LET HIM!!!

Modeling Goodness!

JOURNAL

Day 44
Journey ~ A WOW Factor!

I woke up this morning and I was reminded of what I used to recite in a women's Bible study I attended. Every time we met we would close with, *"Wherever I am God is; the light of God surrounds me, the LOVE of God enfolds me, the POWER of God protects me, the PRESENCE of God watches over me, wherever I am. . .GOD IS!"*

So many times in life I truly believe that we forget or don't acknowledge the fact that we are never alone. We don't walk alone when our day feels dark because God's light surrounds us. We don't walk alone when our hearts may have been broken, because the LOVE of God enfolds us. We don't walk alone when we feel powerless to fix or change a situation, why because the POWER of God protects us. We never walk alone when we are scared and not sure of what to do, because the PRESENCE of God watches over us. Wherever we are, GOD IS! WOW . . . WE ARE NEVER ALONE!

Modeling Goodness!

JOURNAL

_____
_____
_____
_____
_____
_____
_____
_____
_____
_____
_____
_____
_____
_____
_____
_____
_____
_____
_____
_____
_____

Day 45
Journey ~ Relationship!

It amazes me how God knows, one of my favorite things in life is to hear the birds singing. And although I hear them today, there is a feeling of something is just not quite right. I know I am not the only one who has those days. . .God really does know us, he sent me an amazing text through one of my Sister's in another state, everything I have read he has soothed my inner soul and addresses my innermost hurt this morning. Having a relationship with someone means they sense when you need some encouragement and love. . .Thank you God for knowing me and giving me a little more Hope, Love and strength to hang on to! WOW What a mighty God we serve, who has reminded me once again, I Am Wonderfully and Fearfully Made!!!

AND SO ARE YOU!!! Talk to God he Knows!!!

Modeling Goodness!

JOURNAL

Day 46
Journey ~ Forgiveness!

Usually when the word, "forgiveness," is mentioned most people don't immediately think about who they need to forgive. What person has wronged me that I need to let off the hook? Who is it that I need to forgive that does not even know I was offended by them? Although those thoughts are good, what about the forgiveness you may owe yourself? As I have mentioned in many posts, this year has been an experience I will always remember. It brought about a lot of pain, questions and now joy. One of the questions that came up for me was, "Why do I owe myself forgiveness in this situation?" I realized forgiveness was needed for myself as part of the process. So I can see the situation for exactly what it is and learn what I need to do differently to protect me going forward. So, do you need forgiveness from YOU? Hmmm… think about it!

No matter what I have done or what circumstances influenced me, I can start anew, make amends, and accept God's forgiveness. I embrace a new vision of life, and I am free now to express it.

Psalm 130:4 -*There is forgiveness with you*

Modeling Goodness!

JOURNAL

_____

_____

_____

_____

_____

_____

_____

_____

_____

_____

_____

_____

_____

_____

_____

_____

_____

_____

_____

_____

_____

_____

_____

Day 47
Journey ~ What is your DREAM?

I have many dreams and for most of my life I thought that they were only DREAMS, but as my life has progressed, I am learning more and more those dreams are in my heart for a reason. Many of them have come to fruition and some are in the balance, waiting for the right season to step out. DREAMS. . . THEY ARE REAL! Never give up on them. I believe it is how God shows us a glimpse of our purpose! Happy DREAMING!

The Daily Word (*August 28, 2013*-My Dreams) said it like this and I LOVED IT! *My Dreams WITH FAITH, I FOLLOW MY DREAMS. The Rev. Dr. Martin Luther King Jr. once said, "Faith is taking the first step even when you don't see the whole staircase." Dr. King drew on the power of faith to overcome seemingly insurmountable challenges. I have within me this same divine power, and I can use it to pursue my dreams. Whether I dream of writing a book, sailing around the world, or effecting positive change in my community, I, too, must take the first step, even though "the whole staircase" may not be visible. If fear or self-doubt arises, I go within and allow the presence of God to support me in mind, body, and spirit. One step at a time, my way is made clear. With faith, my dreams come to fruition.*

Psalm 146:5,6 *Happy are those whose help is the God of Jacob ... who keeps faith forever.*

Modeling Goodness!

JOURNAL

_____
_____
_____
_____
_____
_____
_____
_____
_____
_____
_____
_____
_____
_____
_____
_____
_____
_____
_____

Day 48
Journey ~ The FIGHT!

I had a conversation yesterday with my clients and my words to them were, "We no longer have to fight in life, we really just need to learn how to respond appropriately."

For many years I can remember always feeling like I was in this fight to prove that I was just as good as...WHOMEVER! Each day depended on *WHOEVER* it was that day, but it definitely was a fight. The problem was, the only person fighting was me, and who I was trying to prove something to, was *ME.* I felt that I needed to prove that I existed. Well, the FIGHT is over. . .I no longer have to prove to ME who I am, I no longer have to prove to ME that I matter, I no longer have to prove to ME that I exist.

Somewhere deep in my heart the reality burst forth, that everybody, anybody already knew all of that, all I needed to do was accept ME! Then I was able to respond to life rather than react!!! What freedom!!!

It is not about fighting the battles of life anymore, it is more about RESPONDING to life APPROPRIATELY and you win no matter the outcome!!!

Modeling Goodness!

JOURNAL

Day 49
Journey ~ What's In Your Heart?

In Proverbs 4:23 is says, *Above all else, guard your heart, for everything you do flows from it.* So, have you guarded your heart, what are you holding in it? Is love there? Is peace there? Is forgiveness there? Is joy there? More importantly, is GOD there? Some of us are so bogged down by the weight of what we won't let go of that we are unable to experience the goodness of our hearts. It is time to let go, learn from the experiences and use the lesson for your greater good! IT WILL BLESS YOU! Not only will it bless you but it will definitely BLESS OTHERS! It's called WISDOM! Free your heart and open it to GOD!

Modeling Goodness!

JOURNAL

_____

_____

_____

_____

_____

_____

_____

_____

_____

_____

_____

_____

_____

_____

_____

_____

_____

_____

_____

_____

_____

_____

_____

Day 50
Journey ~ ...TYGA!

If you are reading this devotional, today is the first day of the rest of your life! Whatever you experienced yesterday, give it to God! He will show you what is next as we walk through each day! Isn't it a blessing to know, no matter how big or small, GOD HAS A PLAN? Isn't it a blessing to know that no matter what we may have gone through it is NO SURPRISE TO HIM? Isn't it a blessing to know, ALL WE HAVE TO DO IS TRUST HIM and do as He guides us to do? Wow, when you think about it, we should never be afraid. His track record in my life has proven that. What does His record look like in yours? THANK YOU GOD ALWAYS (TYGA)!

Modeling Goodness!

JOURNAL

_____
_____
_____
_____
_____
_____
_____
_____
_____
_____
_____
_____
_____
_____
_____
_____
_____
_____
_____
_____
_____
_____
_____

Day 51
Journey ~ The Power of Attraction!

As I began writing this I heard two old sayings in my mind. The first is, "You reap what you sow," and the second was, "Your actions are talking so loud that I can't hear what you're saying."

It is true – people pay more attention to what you do than what you say. That's why the way we live as a child of God is crucial. Those who would dismiss you as a religious fanatic when you try to talk to them about your relationship with this AWESOME GOD, will be unable to ignore your exemplary LIFE. Let them see Jesus in YOU! What they see in you has the POWER TO ATTRACT. Seeing is BELIEVING.

Modeling Goodness!

JOURNAL

Day 52
Journey ~ People Pleaser!

Is that you? Are you a person that at any cost you just want everybody to get along? Do you find it hard to say that huge two-letter word, "NO?" This one word holds so much power, and it can be a huge determining factor in our lives. It can either propel you into an amazing sense of freedom or it can oppress you into a situation that seems to have no end! Many people including myself find it difficult to say, "NO," because of many reasons.

One reason that comes to mind for me is the desire to avoid conflict. Trying to avoid conflict creates conflict by stirring up inner turmoil of not allowing yourself to do or say what you know in your heart needs to be done or said. The fear that if we say, "NO," someone will not like us anymore plays a part whether we admit it or not.

What I have learned is if an individual decides that my ability to live true to myself, is an issue and our friendship is affected by that, then I have to ask the question, "Was that person my friend, *really?*" It is time to take a look at this and find the courage to be true to YOU! Even the Bible says DO IT! You don't believe me? Read this!!!

1 Chronicles 28:20 (KJV) *Be strong and be of good courage, and do it*

JUST DO IT. . .SAY "NO," when "no" is the right answer!

Modeling Goodness!

JOURNAL

_____
_____
_____
_____
_____
_____
_____
_____
_____
_____
_____
_____
_____
_____
_____
_____
_____
_____
_____
_____
_____

Day 53
Journey ~ Are you in Fear?

Are you in fear about something, concerned whether you will have what you need when you need it? When we take the journey back over our lives and are able to see that this is not the first time this fear has shown up. We also see that the outcome was never what we were afraid of happening. The enemy would love to sit us right down in the middle of fear and say those awful words, "I GIVE UP!" But I stopped by this amazing day to say, "Giving up is not an option!"

God has promised to never leave us nor forsake us. He has done it before and guess what? HE WILL DO IT AGAIN! Stand on His PROMISE and our journey will be exactly what we need it to be! HE IS A KEEPER!

Psalm 29:11 *The Lord gives strength to his people; the Lord blesses his people with peace.*

Modeling Goodness!

JOURNAL

Day 54
Journey ~ No Limits!

Have you read the story in the Bible about Jabez in 1 Chronicles 4:9-10? It really sends an amazing message that says, no matter what circumstance you are born into, your life can be more than amazing! Dr. Natalie Francisco stated in her book, I'm Just Saying, "Like Jabez, we can pray and expect God to do what others perhaps thank is impossible once we remove all limitations, whether they are self-improved or otherwise. Israel Houghton's lyrics are powerful, for they remind us not to settle for less than God's best in and for our lives. "No limits; no boundaries. I see increase all around me, stretch forth; break forth. Release me. Enlarge my territory. Say what you heard [from God] so you can see what you said. Take the limits off No limits!"

So No limits, No boundaries WITH GOD HE IS LIMITLESS!!!

Modeling Goodness!

JOURNAL

_____

_____

_____

_____

_____

_____

_____

_____

_____

_____

_____

_____

_____

_____

_____

_____

_____

_____

_____

_____

_____

_____

Day 55
Journey ~ What are you looking for?

Lately, a few people have talked to me about not being sure what it is they are supposed to be doing with their life. Listen, *every* individual has a purpose for living. No one God brings to life on this earth is insignificant. The tragedy of all tragedies is that we should live and die having never found that purpose, that special, God-ordained reason for serving our generation. We have, like no other person on this planet, particular contributions that we are to make in this generation. That contribution may not be as great as your dreams or they might be far beyond your expectations, but whatever they are, you are to find them and carry them out so WHAT ARE YOU LOOKING FOR? Your Purpose is in your Passion!

Model Goodness!

JOURNAL

_____
_____
_____
_____
_____
_____
_____
_____
_____
_____
_____
_____
_____
_____
_____
_____
_____
_____
_____
_____
_____
_____
_____

Day 56
Journey ~ Direction!

As I was reading a devotional today, a thought came to me. "What if you really don't know what to do?" What I mean by that is. Often we have a desire to do whatever it is that God would have to be done. But, in reality you may not know where to start or what it is you are to be doing. I understand that, because although I truly believe there are some things in my life that I believe is part of my purpose. There are times when I wonder if there is something God is trying to tell me and I am missing it. It is truly my desire to hear the words from God one day, as it says in:

"Matthew 25:21 His lord said to him, 'Well done, good and faithful servant; you were faithful over a few things, I will make you ruler over many things. Enter into the joy of your lord."

When you have been given the talent and ability to do something, don't allow fear, laziness, uncertainty or people get in the way of fulfilling that which is for you to do. In your silence and prayer time with God, He says to ask for wisdom and guess what He will give it to you!

Read Matthew 25:20-28 it will encourage you.

Model Goodness!

JOURNAL

Day 57
Journey ~ When Life Hurts!

I stated the following before but it is the memory I have that makes me feel better when life hurts.

I was asked yesterday what was one of my favorite memories and although I could come up with many, like sitting on my knees at the kitchen table as my Grandmother mixed the cake mix made from scratch, waiting for the spoon or the bowl so that I could have what was left. Sometimes, I believe she would leave just a little bit in the bowl just for me. I could say the day I walked across the stage to receive my Bachelor's degree after many years of attempting to complete it. I could have said my favorite memory was the day God blessed me to walk across the stage a second time to receive my Master's degree in Psychology. But what I said instead was one day after many years of being in my drug addiction, and finally getting sober, I was in my one room I was renting, sitting on the side of my bed, one beautiful Saturday morning. I realized I could hear the BIRDS SINGING!

This may not mean anything to anyone, but if you had been where I had been and all you could see was total darkness even in the daytime. There were no Birds singing in my life and if they were I could not hear them what I could hear though was DEATH! Here I am 26 years later still hearing the birds singing! So when you see me post, "I can Hear the birds singing! I choose LIFE not DEATH!!! I want to Model Goodness rather than worthless movement!!! So I ask you, what is your favorite memory? If you don't have one it is not late to create ONE! Choose LIFE!

Deuteronomy 30:19 *I call heaven and earth to witness against you that today I have set before you life or death, blessing or curse. Oh, that you would choose life; that you and your children might live!*

Model Goodness!

JOURNAL

_____
_____
_____
_____
_____
_____
_____
_____
_____
_____
_____
_____
_____
_____
_____
_____
_____
_____
_____
_____
_____
_____
_____
_____

Day 58
Journey ~ Excitement!

This morning I am feeling some excitement in the air. Why you ask, well at the time of writing this, it is July and it is soon to be over. July is the 7th month of the year and I believe that the number 7 is completion. There has been a lot to take place in my life for the last 7 months and if you are like me, we are seeking the end. We have to believe and do what God's Word says in Exodus 4:29, *And the people trusted and listened believing that God was concerned with what was going on with the Israelites and knew all about their affliction. They bowed low and they worshiped.*

If God was concerned about the Israelites, guess what? He is concerned about you and I! So, whatever we may be concerned about on this day, just know that God knows and has a plan for each one of us. JUST BELIEVE YOUR COMPLETION IS ON THE WAY!

Model Goodness!

JOURNAL

Day 59
Journey ~ RIGHT NOW!

Have you ever felt like you wish this very moment, this "right now" was over? Sometimes life feels like it is sooooo hard, when the moments come that seem dark, heavy just plain overwhelming. Well, I have to admit that is exactly how I feel today, and I want so badly to be on the other side of this lesson. But yet I don't want to miss the valuable things that will come out of this. So I stand and attempt to walk through all the way to the blessed place God has for me. If you are feeling like I am feeling today, I want you to know that THIS TOO SHALL PASS! Not because we make it pass but because it passes in GOD, and He is ready to move us to the next lesson! He leads us beside still waters, He restores our soul!

At this very moment if we are not present we miss the experiences we need at that moment. It holds the needs for our movement forward. It contains what we need to minister to those God has ordained for our path. We must feel all that there is to feel, experience all there is to experience to become all that God has ordained for us to be.

So, let's stay focused and learn the lessons of today, and we will be prepared for the journey and joys of tomorrow.

Be here now. This is the only place you need to be. And from this place, all things are possible!

Model Goodness!

JOURNAL

Day 60
JOURNEY ~ What Do You Do When You Don't Know What To Do?

I was always taught, when you don't know what to do, do nothing! That sounds good and in the past I have found it to be a good thing for me. Right now in experiencing the grief process of my father, doing nothing feels excruciating. On the other side, I don't have a clue on what to do. I have realized that I don't know how to really handle the process of grief. I know I am sad, but yet I am really not sure what that is suppose to look like, when I am alone or with others. One thing I do know, I don't want to NOT GRIEVE. I don't want to act as if everything is okay. I don't want to delay what is inevitable. I don't have the answer YET on how to handle this. So, JOURNEY with me and let's find out together, one day you might need this!

Model Goodness!

JOURNAL

_____
_____
_____
_____
_____
_____
_____
_____
_____
_____
_____
_____
_____
_____
_____
_____
_____
_____
_____
_____
_____

Day 61
Journey ~ Loving Others!

As I think about how we should love others, it came to me that there are some people who do not understand love and will reject it. Does that mean we stop loving them? What if God made a decision to stop loving us when we did not understand how much He loved us and rejected that love? He didn't, He keeps loving us in spite of us and we must do the same. Jesus' ultimate sacrifice of laying down His life so that all humanity could experience eternal life showed true devotion. His willingness to go to the cross gave us the opportunity to experience an intimacy with God that was not available before. Likewise, we can honor others with the same love. That strength and power of love resides within us. God gave us the ability to show His love to everyone we meet. In Romans 12:10 it says, *Be devoted to one another in brotherly love. Honor one another above yourselves.*

Therefore, Be Bold! Be Courageous! Love Like Jesus does! IT IS IN US!

Model Goodness!

JOURNAL

_____
_____
_____
_____
_____
_____
_____
_____
_____
_____
_____
_____
_____
_____
_____
_____
_____
_____
_____
_____
_____

Day 62
Journey ~ Here Comes the Judge!

In each of our lives we have experienced things that we have made a judgment about whether that judgment is a good one or a bad one. Whether it is a judgment of someone else or of ourselves the latter judgment is the one that I have found to be the most silent and the one that I didn't realize for a while. Judging myself or ourselves negatively due to our experiences can delay us from seeing the TRUTH! It delays us from dealing with what we need to at the time. This does not mean we may not have a part, but that's it right there, we have a PART not a WHOLE! So remember KEEP THE MAIN THING THE MAIN THING. Proverbs 3:5-6 reminds us to, *Trust in the Lord with all your heart; do not depend on your own understanding. Seek his will in all you do, and he will show you which path to take.*

Model Goodness!

JOURNAL

_____
_____
_____
_____
_____
_____
_____
_____
_____
_____
_____
_____
_____
_____
_____
_____
_____
_____
_____
_____

Day 63
Journey~ I AM WHO I AM!

I often say to others that everything I have experienced in my life, the good, the bad and the indifferent are ALL JEWELS. They are jewels for me to share my lessons good, bad or indifferent with others, that they too can find the jewels in their lives to help others. Guess what? YOU HAVE JEWELS TOO! Stop sweeping them under your rug! The Daily Word (Harmony-July 1, 2013) expressed it this way:

MY GIFTS ARE AN ESSENTIAL PART OF DIVINE HARMONY. *On the day I was born, I brought a unique song into the world. It is a song only I can express—a divine manifestation. It is essential to the great oneness of us all. No puzzle is finished without all the pieces, and no melody is complete without all the notes. If I withhold the talents that are mine to give, I create an incomplete harmony in the world. If I try to make myself a copy of someone else, I create disharmony within myself. God has blessed us all with gifts, and I celebrate mine. No one else has my smile, my laughter, my love, or my voice. As I share from God, I find nothing lacking. I give freely in harmony with the good that God provides for me and for us all.*

1 Corinthians 12:7- *To each is given the manifestation of the Spirit for the common good.*

Model Goodness!

JOURNAL

_____
_____
_____
_____
_____
_____
_____
_____
_____
_____
_____
_____
_____
_____
_____
_____
_____
_____
_____
_____
_____
_____

Day 64
Journey ~ PROTECTION!

In today's world there are so many things we need to be protected from. Life can be so overwhelming from the actions of others who have no principles or convictions in their heart. That makes us want to lash out or do things that are not truly in our character. What we need to do is pray and be still and watch the hand of the Lord move in our favor. Isaiah 52:12 it says, *The Lord your God will lead you and protect you on every side.*

We all have fears – fear of harm, fear of losing a child, fear of being alone, and fear of failure. When our fears rise up and threaten to overcome us. When we feel sick in the pit of our stomach and our heart aches with anxiety remember this: God is with you, every day, every hour, every moment. Focus on Him, really focus, and we will see that our fears are nothing more than speculation that is swept away in His presence. Where the Spirit of the Lord is, there is liberty!

Model Goodness!

JOURNAL

_____

_____

_____

_____

_____

_____

_____

_____

_____

_____

_____

_____

_____

_____

_____

_____

_____

_____

_____

_____

_____

_____

_____

Day 65
Journey ~ Don't Worry!

In our lives we have been given everything we need to move forward on our journey. Although there may be times when it may appear that we are in need, God's Word reminds us in Matthew 6:25-26, *Therefore I say to you, do not worry about your life, what you will eat or what you will drink; nor about your body, what you will put on. Is not life more than food and the body more than clothing? Look at the birds of the air, for they neither sow nor reap nor gather into barns; yet your heavenly Father feeds them. Are you not of more value than they?* We are valuable to God and no matter what it may look like our needs will be met!

So, what do you believe about today? No matter what you may believe, one thing is clear, God already knows, He already knows what we will face today, and He knows that we are ready. Why? Because He placed it on our path. He knows what we will think, He knows what we will do, He knows the outcome before it even happens. So, if we profess to love this amazing God who KNOWS waaaaaaay before we do, then what we should consider is, we may not understand, but we must trust HIM! He knows that today is going to be amazing, so let him do it!

Father, You have words that show us Your way of walking in obedience to Thee. Ways that may seem unreasonable at times to our limited brains, but ways that are filled with Thy purpose and wisdom. Father, only You can see beyond our day today and only You can prepare us to walk ever closer to Thee. Amen and Amen!

Model Goodness with PEACE!!!

JOURNAL

Day 66
Journey ~ Feelings!

When I first began writing "Journey," I think somewhere I felt I just wanted to bless others, which is true. I believe I did not include myself in the equation, and trust me I need to be included! My journey in the last 7 to 8 months has been an experience I will be able to grow from for a long time. One of the things I have learned most is that I HAVE to allow myself to feel what comes, NO SWEEPING UNDER THE RUG!

In Ecclesiastes 7:14 it says, *When times are good, be happy; but when times are bad, consider: God has made the one as well as the other.* WOW, we may tend to think of God gratefully in the good times and ask for His help in the bad. But sometimes we have to consider that God brings good out of both. No matter what our feelings tell us, we can trust Him to work out His purpose in us at all times. God isn't bound by our feelings, He is bound by His Word. God doesn't want to stifle our emotions because they allow us to feel His love, His compassion, and His joy. He wants to help us harness, control and use the power of our feelings to bless the Kingdom. Therefore, we should not be bound by our feelings either but by His PROMISES!

Model Goodness!

JOURNAL

Day 67
Journey ~ Do You Respect You?

Respect means something different from one person to another. Webster defines respect in 9 different ways – no wonder we don't really have a clear picture of what the word really means. I can tell you what I believe respect means and I can guarantee it would be different from someone else. In Proverbs 11:16 it says, *A kindhearted woman/man gains respect.*

I believe that as we grow in God, we begin to demonstrate His character and nature in our thoughts, attitudes, and behavior. Through us, His GOODNESS becomes evident to others, and their respect for us increases. This will happen not because we demand it but because it is a natural response to God's glory. For the same reason, we must RESPECT OURSELVES and cast down thoughts of inferiority and unworthiness. RESPECT God's presence at work within YOU! *Being confident of this, that He who began a good work in you will carry it on to completion until the day of Christ Jesus.* (Phil. 1:6) There is a lot of GOOD IN YOU!

Model Goodness!!

JOURNAL

_____

_____

_____

_____

_____

_____

_____

_____

_____

_____

_____

_____

_____

_____

_____

_____

_____

_____

_____

_____

_____

_____

Day 68
Journey ~ YOU!!!

How okay are you really with who you are? When you find out that YOU were not on the invitation list for a party of someone you know, how do you feel? When you feel like you are being rejected by others do you feel it is because of YOU? Do you sit back and wonder why you don't fit in the circles of some that you see? Well, let me first say that even if all of that is true for YOU, my answer to that is . . . IT'S REALLY OKAY!! It's Okay that you were not on the invitation list, and as a special lady I know said recently, "If you feel you have been rejected it does not mean it is something wrong with YOU!" I remember someone saying, "rejection means to be thrown away, and no one has the power to do that, unless you give it to them." So those circles you think you would like to fit in, is not your circle. But there is one available for YOU, which we sometimes don't recognize because of paying attention to the circles that are not for YOU!

Listen, living this life we live can be difficult, and I don't have all of the answers on how to truly change how we feel about certain things. But what I do know for sure is, I may not get on the list, I may not fit in the circle and I have and will be rejected from time to time. But I know for a fact that I am on God's list! He always sends an invitation to spend time with him. His circle has no rejection and He brings those together that celebrate rather than tolerate each other if YOU let Him!

Model Goodness!

JOURNAL

_____
_____
_____
_____
_____
_____
_____
_____
_____
_____
_____
_____
_____
_____
_____
_____
_____
_____
_____
_____
_____
_____
_____
_____

Day 69
Journey ~ MY HELP!

One of my favorite movies is, "The Help," and I enjoyed it so much because there were many lessons in the movie. One of the most important lessons was the willingness to go to any length to help another human being, and then the human being accepting the help! Psalm 33:20 says *Our soul waits for the Lord; He is our help and our shield.*

Just like in the movie we wait for help and when God sends it, we have to be open to receive it. So, who do you turn to when trouble comes your way? We're blessed if we have faithful friends and loved ones here on earth. But whether we have such support in our lives or not, God has promised we will never face adversity alone again and again in the Bible. He declares His desire to help us. Even when no one else is there He will be, and He has limitless resources. No matter what our needs, call on Him. GOD'S RESOURCES NEVER RUN OUT! Are you open to receive HIM?

Model Goodness!

JOURNAL

Day 70
Journey ~ FRIENDSHIP!

As we go through life, there are some very important elements I believe makes the journey easier. One of those elements is whom we travel with. We don't live on an island as much as some would like to think they journey all by themselves. I have to say that total isolation was not the plan or order for our lives. God intended us to fellowship with one another. If that were not true, He would not have said in Matthew 18:20, *Where two or three COME TOGETHER in my name, there am I with them.* So, who are you traveling with?

The individuals we *Journey* with in life can either make us or break us. How does someone make us? Well they are the individuals who are friend enough to be there for you, who love you enough to share the truth rather then make you feel good. So what is the break us part? Well, that is those individuals who tear you down, never celebrate you, and no matter how much you try they can find fault in all that you do. When you walk away you feel worse than you did when you came together. Since we are not on an island, our prayers should be for discernment of who we are traveling with. . .remember this, you don't have to dance with everyone, but you must dance with someone!

Model Goodness! LOL

JOURNAL

Day 71
Journey ~ SELF!

Have you ever felt like you did not recognize who you were? Asked yourself, "How did I get to this place?" As if you lost a part of SELF and you were not quite sure when it happened. I am convinced there is power in taking care of SELF!

I remember reading how there is nothing more powerful in the world than our ability to understand the spirit of our true selves. The spirit of self teaches us and lead us to the desires of our dreams and purpose. It understands what we some time forget, how amazing we are, that we are whole and complete. It is aware of our abilities to do that which has been ordained for us to do. So what is the message in this? The message is, we have exactly what we need to be, to do, to live, standing in the power of the Holy Spirit. The spirit of self, which outweighs any other being. The source of our power, the Holy Spirit who guides us to our higher good, our higher greatness! So, I dare you, I double dutch dare you to TAKE CARE OF SELF!!!

It is time to call SELF back to you for the POWER OF YOUR PURPOSE!

Model Goodness!

JOURNAL

Day 72
Journey ~ Challenges!

Somewhere in my thought process I was hoping that as I got older the challenges of life would get less. Although the types of challenges are different from what my younger days look like, I still have to determine how to deal with what comes before me. Some of my most recent challenges remind me of the saying, "Life will continue to give you the lesson until you learn it." So, if you are like me in dealing with life's challenges, remember we are able to find peace in the midst of it all. Why? Well, because I believe what the Word of God says in Hebrews 12:1-2 *Let us run with endurance the race that is set before us, looking unto Jesus the author and finisher of our faith.*

So, Life is full of challenges. While some are short-term, others last a lifetime. What keeps us determined and motivated? Do we seek the help of others or prefer to go at it alone? We may want to take a toddler's approach to these challenges. As a toddler ventures into walking, he or she takes one step at a time, with help from a steady adult or an available piece of furniture. Eventually, they walk on their own. With God's help, take life's challenges one step at a time. God will walk beside us and give us strength to overcome whatever is on our journey! All we have to do is TRUST HIM!

Model Goodness!

JOURNAL

_____
_____
_____
_____
_____
_____
_____
_____
_____
_____
_____
_____
_____
_____
_____
_____
_____
_____
_____
_____
_____

Day 73
Journey ~ Do You LOVE YOU?

We experience many things in our lives and through it all much of what we experience can take a toll on how we view ourselves and how we love ourselves. So do you love YOU? No matter what, love yourself, LOVE YOURSELF, even if it looks like the world around you is irked with you. Love yourself even if it feels like those you've counted on most have gone away. Love yourself even if you wonder if God has abandoned you. When it feels like the journey has stopped, the magic is gone, and you've been left sitting on the curb, LOVE YOURSELF. When you're confused and angry about how things are going or how they've gone, LOVE YOURSELF.

No matter what happens or where you are, LOVE YOURSELF. It doesn't matter if you aren't certain where you're going or if there's any place left to go, LOVE YOURSELF. This situation will change, this time will pass, and the magic will return. So will joy and faith. You will feel connected again to yourself, God, the universe, and life, but the first thing to do is to pray and LOVE YOURSELF. All the good you want will follow.

1 Corinthians 13:8, *Love never ends. 13:13, And now these three remain: faith, hope and love. But the greatest of these is love.*

Model Goodness!

JOURNAL

_____
_____
_____
_____
_____
_____
_____
_____
_____
_____
_____
_____
_____
_____
_____
_____
_____
_____
_____
_____
_____
_____

Day 74
Journey ~ WHO YOU MAD AT?

Did you know that unexpressed anger is like cancer? Hiding it, tucking it away deep inside is not the answer. Not feeling anger won't make it go away but its energy will still be there, pounding away inside us and in subtle ways, pounding away at others, too. Anger will keep us off balance, on edge, and irritable until we acknowledge our anger, feel it, and release it. So many times we have a conversation with someone and walk away asking, "Why is he or she so angry?"

We need to give ourselves permission to feel all of our emotions, including anger. That doesn't mean lashing out at people, it means finding what works for you appropriately. Find ways to express your anger with grace and dignity. Anger can help us to get to the next place in our lives if it is used correctly. Feeling and expressing our anger in appropriate ways will take us forward to a place of power within ourselves. Knowing where to go and not go in dealing with anger is a way to learn what it is trying to teach you, it can be a great guide if you use it right!

Model Goodness!

JOURNAL

Day 75
Journey ~When You Don't Know What to Say

As I write this morning I am not really sure what it is I want or need to say, but I am committed to sharing on Journey each day, so let's see what God gives me. I have read a couple of things this morning one made me cry and another reminded me how I get through the parts of life that feel difficult. The first was about giving myself the freedom to wear out my beliefs. What beliefs am I talking about? Well, the beliefs that are sabotaging our ability to be happy, joyous, and free! Parts of our journey in life will take us through places, through people, and through our beliefs. We wear these beliefs out one by one, shedding them and making room for a little more light. We need to look around at our lives and realize we can trust where we are. Trust what we're going through. Some belief is wearing thin right now, and only you can say when it is time to throw out that belief.

In the second reading, a verse was used, that says to me that no matter what I believe, God is still God and in control. Why? Because Hebrews 11:13 says, *What is seen was made from things that are not visible.* So, if you are in the process of wearing out a belief, then please do it with FAITH! With faith we can do all things. With faith, I am whole in body, mind, and spirit. With faith, I know that nothing is impossible. Whatever my goals or aspirations, I accomplish them through faith in the power of God within me. My faith is solid, for God is my strength, my understanding, and my constant companion. Therefore, with Faith I can become who God has planned me to become!

Model Goodness!

JOURNAL

Day 76
Journey ~ Grace!

At the time of writing this, it is the first day of a new month, the fifth month of the year, and I heard for many years that the number five is the number of grace. So what is grace really? Well, I am so glad you asked! Grace is often defined as God's unmerited favor. It means that His love, care, and concern for us are all free gifts – we haven't earned them. What a wonderful thing to be loved and accepted JUST BECAUSE!

In God's eyes, we are already pretty enough, handsome enough, smart enough, good enough to receive His best. He wants us to become all we were created to be, but our relationship with Him doesn't hinge on it. What a wonderful word, "GRACE" is!

Model Goodness!

JOURNAL

_____

_____

_____

_____

_____

_____

_____

_____

_____

_____

_____

_____

_____

_____

_____

_____

_____

_____

_____

_____

Day 77
Journey ~ GOT Comfort?

In 2 Corinthians 1:4 it says what I have experienced for myself true comfort: *He comforts us in all our troubles so that we can comfort others. When they are troubled, we will be able to give them the same comfort God has given us.*

Never discount where you are, your place of discomfort could very well be exactly what you need to comfort others. Don't miss the blessing of allowing your comfort to come by ignoring, dismissing, refusing to walk through and/or sweeping it under the rug! Nothing, absolutely nothing happens by mistakes, it does not take God by surprise. So, because He already knows, He is always ready to COMFORT!

What is comfort? Comfort soothes the spirit within, it has the ability to renew our power and assuredness. Comfort allows you to be you through the power of your spirit.

GOT COMFORT??? Model Goodness!

ESTHER RENEE' WRIGHT

JOURNAL

_____
_____
_____
_____
_____
_____
_____
_____
_____
_____
_____
_____
_____
_____
_____
_____
_____
_____
_____
_____
_____
_____

Day 78
Journey ~ Do You Know What You Want?

There are many of us who have desires and dreams, but because they feel or look so BIG we dismiss them and never move toward them. When you think about some possible reasons why we are guilty of this, the first thing that comes to me is, fear of failure. We are so afraid that going after that big dream or desire is going to make me look like a fool if it doesn't work out – wrong answer! Secondly, we sometimes turn inward unconsciously, thinking, "What makes me think I can do that?" The truth is, you can't by yourself, but GOD CAN!

Read what Melody Beattie said about this:
Have you ever asked yourself the question, What do I want? Have you ever wondered how the things or things you want would be like? Are you really passionate about the current events of your life that you are exerting all of your energy to right now? Well, if you take the opportunity to create the images of your desires in your mind, it is the first step toward moving towards your the dream that has been there all along. It was predestined!

So, believe it! You can have what you want, don't be afraid to look at that dream you desire straight in the face. You have to see it before it can BE!

Model Goodness!

JOURNAL

_____

_____

_____

_____

_____

_____

_____

_____

_____

_____

_____

_____

_____

_____

_____

_____

_____

_____

_____

_____

_____

_____

Day 79
Journey ~ From Fear to Joy!

Wow, last week for me when I look back was amazing. It was amazing because I actually made very important decision I needed to make and have been afraid to make. What power I have found in doing what I need to do and better take care of myself. Someone said to me one day that, they did not understand why people think that doing what is best for you is suppose to feel good! When we have to make changes in our lives that are best for us we won't move if it appears to hurt rather than empower! I feel empowered and did it hurt but on the other side of that came the gift! What are you afraid of that if you did what you *need* to do it looks like it would hurt? Don't miss the awesome gift that awaits you!

I have experienced that when I allow myself to look my fears dead in the face, my life shifts. It shifts into the place of empowerment to do the thing I was so afraid I could not do. I realized my fear counts on me to not look at it, why? Because the enemy is really afraid of me if I do!!!

Model Goodness!

JOURNAL

_____

_____

_____

_____

_____

_____

_____

_____

_____

_____

_____

_____

_____

_____

_____

_____

_____

_____

_____

_____

_____

_____

_____

Day 80
Journey ~ Who Loves YOU?

This morning I was on Pinterest and I saw a picture that mentioned self-love. I immediately thought, "Why is it that we so often don't think about how important that is?" I really believe that somewhere I got the wrong message about loving and taking care of me. Maybe you did too. Somehow, I got the message that if I loved me; it would mean I thought too highly of myself. So for years I attempted to put that self-love fire out, and see myself as just mediocre. When in fact I was and am AMAZING, and guess what, SO ARE YOU! Then I picked up the books I read every morning and what did Melody Beattie talk about for today? Well let me show you how God talks to me:

We need to fall in love with ourselves. We are good at being kind and loving with others, but it is time to be kind and loving with ourselves. Each day we should be aware of our personal needs, and take care of what we can. When we allow ourselves to feel self loved, we are able to live better, feel better, love better. When this magic happens, God's love happens!

NOW THAT'S WHAT I'M TALKING ABOUT. GOD IS AMAZING and HE MADE US TO BE AS WELL! DO YOU BOO!

Model Goodness!

JOURNAL

Day 81
Journey ~ Have you had a Mary and Elizabeth experience?

I know you are saying, "What is she talking about now?" Well, in the Bible it tells us how when Mary went to see Elizabeth the baby she was carrying leaped. I believe we can have that same experience with the people that we meet on the journey we travel each day. I also believe that we often miss this experience, why? We miss the experience for many reasons but a couple of reasons that come to mind for me is: one, we tend to forget that what happened during the Bible days is still possible for today. Secondly, I think we just don't pay attention to our experiences.

I remember having a conversation with an individual and he said, "I feel your vibration." At first I did not understand what he was saying. Then he explained, we all have this energy that when two people honestly connect they cross and feed off of each other. So, I began to pay more attention to the energy I feel when I meet and interact with others. This observation allows me to be conscious of who I am journeying with, and how their energy makes me feel. I have come to the understanding that I will not connect with everyone's energy. But, I love it when I meet someone and when I walk away I feel good as a result of our energy crossing. I seek the energy of love and when that happens I call that my amazing Mary and Elizabeth experience!

Luke 1:41 - *And it occurred that when Elizabeth heard Mary's greeting, the baby leaped in her womb, and Elizabeth was filled with and controlled by the Holy Spirit.*

The Mary and Elizabeth experience is REAL!

Model Goodness!

JOURNAL

Day 82
Journey

I was sitting thinking about how caring for others may feel outside of what is normal. Sometimes I feel that I care for people more than I should, but it hit me – JESUS DIED because of His love for people. He experienced pain because it was the only way for those He loved could be set free! His being beaten and hung on a cross was not for SHOW it was for LOVE! I think I will keep caring and loving others FOR LOVE NOT FOR SHOW!

Model Goodness!

JOURNAL

Day 83
Journey ~ Change Your Perspective!

So many times in life things happen and if we let them they can consume our every thought, behavior, and many other aspects of our being. In the consumption many things can be missed, most importantly we bring about the opportunity to miss life and the awesome journey God has prepared for us to take. I read the Daily Word this morning and it talked about praying, I absolutely love the title that was used, *"I pray for you and surround you with love."*

When life shows up in the uncomfortable ways that it can at times, do what we have been taught to do. PRAY! God is not surprised life showed up the way it has, HE KNOWS THE PLANS HE HAS FOR US! So change your perspective, and stop fighting that which you cannot change.

Daily Word (Pray for Others, August 15, 2014): *"Pray for Others, I PRAY FOR YOU AND SURROUND YOU WITH LOVE. Prayer is a gift I give myself and others. When I pray, I commune with God and the Love that enfolds us all. Praying for others not only opens my heart, but touches the hearts of those individuals as well. We are united in God. When I pray, I do not focus on particular needs or wants. I pray for a greater awareness of God. This helps my loved ones and me through any challenge. The power of God evokes change in every life. I affirm God's goodness as I pray. The root of all prayer is love – love for God, love for self, love for others. In an awareness of God's unending love, I pray for others, knowing that each person is filled with and surrounded by Love."*

1 Corinthians 13:13 - *Now faith, hope, and love abide, these three; and the greatest of these is love.*

PRAY INSTEAD and MODEL GOODNESS!

JOURNAL

Day 84
Journey ~ Where Do I Fit!!!

Many days of my life I have wondered where do I fit. Because many days I was not sure. Therefore, I often found myself on a quest to figure that out. It wasn't a conscious quest, but I noticed that I was trying to place myself in the lives of others that I believe I wanted to be a part of. Only to discover not only did I not feel comfortable once I sat on their row, but they were not receptive to myself placement. I would walk away feeling some kind of way, (rejected) but not realizing at the time, not fitting there was a gift. A gift to allow God to place me on or create the row in my life where fitting was without question. So what am I saying, stop pushing a square peg into a round a hole. . . IT WON'T FIT!

Pray and ask God to lead you to creating your fits in life, He already knows what that looks like. . . Just for YOU!!!

Modeling Goodness!

JOURNAL

_____
_____
_____
_____
_____
_____
_____
_____
_____
_____
_____
_____
_____
_____
_____
_____
_____
_____
_____
_____
_____
_____

Day 85
Journey ~ Passion!

At the time of writing this entry, it is Passion Week and I wonder how many of us are really giving that much thought. Do we truly understand what this week means, and why it had to happen? Do we really understand the reason for Jesus' walk on this earth? In case you are one who is wondering what all the hoopla is about, then consider that Jesus came that we may have life, and have life more abundantly! He revealed His passion for us in the suffering He willingly went through on our behalf. His passion for us put in place what true love and forgiveness is all about. We are able to live and not be perfect. We are free to love and be loved. We are permitted to be who God created us to be. WE ARE FREE!

Life is more than setbacks, and it's not static. Appreciate and respect where you are now. But let yourself move to the next level when its time. Celebrate your breakthroughs when they come. Listen to that quiet voice, that fleeting thought that says, 'why don't you?' Even if it's something you have never done before. LIVE that is why Jesus died that we may LIVE!

Model Goodness!

JOURNAL

Day 86
Journey ~ Being Our Best!

Life has been for me lately, really REAL! It is as if I can stick my hand out and touch it. Experiencing some things that almost feel surreal. What is amazing to me about this is the willingness to seek truth and positive ways to use what has been presented. Instead of letting it take me under! Have you found yourself doing life instead of life doing YOU? I believe that is what happens when we say "yes," to God rather than running away!

In John 1:43 it says, *Jesus decided to go to Galilee, He found Philip and said to him, follow me.* Due to the willingness to live life based on the will of God, we can find ourselves in an awesome position to be bold and move beyond our comfort zones. We become unlimited with resources on matters large and small. Why? Because within us lies all the wisdom and capabilities we need to be successful. We can be confident of the good results that come from the Spirit of God expressing through each and every one of us. So remember my expression may not look like your expression, BUT IT'S ALL GOD and GOOD!

Model Goodness!

JOURNAL

_____
_____
_____
_____
_____
_____
_____
_____
_____
_____
_____
_____
_____
_____
_____
_____
_____
_____
_____
_____
_____
_____

Day 87
Journey ~ THIS DAY*!*

The birds are singing outside my window this morning even before the sun has peeked out from behind the clouds. They are up and ready to do what is theirs to do on this day! So, am I also up and ready to do what is mine to do on this day? Am I ready to take this day on with great enthusiasm? Which means, if you don't already know, *with God!*

Seek your purpose for THIS DAY. I bet it could be amazing if you want it to be. Each day we are allowed to do what is ours to do. There is great purpose and amazing value in every step we take. We should be more aware of the assignments being given to us. Seek what it is God has allowed us to wake up and do. Embrace that God has you in mind when He touches you each morning. Do what is yours to do!!!

There is purpose there!

Model Goodness!

JOURNAL

Day 88
Journey ~ When life REALLY shows UP!!!

I have not been writing lately on this page because, as the title says, LIFE HAS SHOWN UP FOR REAL in my life. The words just have not been coming to me, to express in the way to be meaningful to you. But, what I can say is, I have been holding on to everything I know in my heart to be true. And the truth is. . .God loves me, He will not leave me nor forsake me. God will provide me and my family the strength to finish this JOURNEY of what appears to be my Father's transition. It has been a long road these last 3 months, but yet we stand and continue to TRUST GOD!

If you are dealing with LIFE at this very moment, I want to share with you that in spite of how I feel, I know in my heart that this is going to be okay. Even if it ends totally opposite of what my family may desire. The last truth I want to share with you is this: God's will is perfect!!!

Model Goodness!

JOURNAL

_____

_____

_____

_____

_____

_____

_____

_____

_____

_____

_____

_____

_____

_____

_____

_____

_____

_____

_____

_____

Day 89
Journey ~ Restoration

I decided to make this weekend my restoration weekend. To rest, be lazy, to do whatever I felt like doing or not doing. In this rest time I have had an opportunity to think about a lot of things, but the most prevalent thought was, how blessed I am. I have realized at the very moment God thought of my existence, I was headed for greatness! Every blessing I have received and will receive is my birthright. . .He pre-destined it that way!!!

Wow how awesome is that? The moment I became an idea in God's mind, I was blessed. That tells me God loves us beyond measure, He guides us and provides for us. What is so exciting about this is no one and I mean NO ONE can withhold my blessings, or yours, for they are God given and there is only ONE GOD! I thank God with everything in my heart. I AM SOOOOO BLESSED! And So are YOU!

Model Goodness!

JOURNAL

_____
_____
_____
_____
_____
_____
_____
_____
_____
_____
_____
_____
_____
_____
_____
_____
_____
_____
_____
_____
_____
_____

Day 90
Journey ~ Your Talents?

Your Talents! I love the saying, "Before God at the end of my life, I would hope that I would not have a single bit of talent left, and could say, I used everything YOU gave me." It reminded me of my Pastor Remus E. Wright and Myles Monroe both of which I heard this same thought from. It made me wonder, how many of us have talents we are not using? And why? A whole list of reasons have come to me, and one of the reasons that bothers me most. Is how we can allow the actions and rejection of others to control our ability to move forward. We are so attached to what others opinions are of us, when in fact their opinion truly is not the fuel that should matter. We have allowed the gifts that God has placed inside of us to lay dormant, because someone else may not approve. Or someone else's talent looks like it is so much more or SOMETHING. Or someone else said we couldn't do it and would never do it. . . REALLY???

The only opinion that matters is the opinion of God. He made us and He knows what we can and cannot do. . . BECAUSE HE PUT IT THERE!!! The opinion of others will never bless you like the OPINION OF GOD!!!

Model Goodness!

JOURNAL

_____

_____

_____

_____

_____

_____

_____

_____

_____

_____

_____

_____

_____

_____

_____

_____

_____

_____

_____

_____

_____

_____

Day 91
Journey ~ PEACE!

When I started writing this my soul felt calm, serene, quiet, and smooth like still water. Then I realized how fast one can lose it because I lost this in my computer four times, in my quest to share this message with you! I won't give up! I can remember when that quiet feeling would scare me, why? Because, I didn't recognize what it was. I said to a friend of mine, "I don't like this feeling like *nothing is happening in my life* feeling."

She said, "God has granted you some peace and you don't know what to do with it."

She was so right! Today I do know what to do with it – Enjoy every second of it, because just like anything in life, this too shall pass.

Peace is to the Kingdom of God what oxygen is to the atmosphere. Considering this truth, you may be wondering why you so often feel agitated and anxious. Think of it this way. Though oxygen permeates the air around us, we must breathe it into our lungs for it to do us any good. We must choose to let God rule in our heart. We must invite Him in. As we open our hearts to Him the PEACE will follow!

Model Goodness!

JOURNAL

Day 92
Journey ~ Keep it Moving!

There is something I really want to share with you this morning, which I believe is important. The first thing is **we are human** first! We make mistakes, we may go in and out of faith, sometimes we say things that may not be the right thing to say. There may be even days where we feel stuck and it seems like we can't get it going. Why? Because WE ARE HUMAN! How would we do what we are mandated to do if our lives were perfect? Where would our awesome testimonies come from if we never experienced anything?

There is purpose, meaning, and rhythm to each step, each mistake, each conversation, and each feeling. Each one is another step on our journey! If you've lost your way and can't find life's rhythm, don't worry. In Psalm 16:11 it says, *you show me the path of life. In your presence there is fullness of joy.*

Just keep it moving, and keep your heart open and you will STEP INTO IT! The presence of God, the fullness of joy, and along with it, the rest of your journey!

Model Goodness!

JOURNAL

Day 93
Journey ~ What does it mean to you to have PATIENCE for real?

I read the Daily Word, June 24, 2014, and it put this in a perspective I have never thought of before. So I thought I would share it with you, I pray it blesses you as it blessed me:

Patience is an act of confidence that all is unfolding as it should—even when the process takes longer than I had hoped or expected.

Patience is not laziness or indifference. I don't have to push or force a result in order to feel as if I am making progress. But just as a farmer cannot hurry or worry a harvest into existence, I cannot rush results that must unfold in their own time.

True patience is a silent energy, one that restores and strengthens. I deny power to any feelings of doubt or impatience, and while I wait, I pray. I stay focused on the present moment, comforted by a quiet faith, and patiently expecting the greater good to come.

May you be made strong … and may you be prepared to endure everything with patience.—Colossians 1:11

Awwwww Patience. . . PRICELESS PEACE!

Model Goodness!

JOURNAL

Day 94
Journey ~ Wish Them Well!

WOW, what a LOVE WEEK it was. Today I had the opportunity to watch eight of my clients all of them 17 years old, graduate with their GED and be released after being locked down for the last 90 days. In thinking about this, I wonder what we need to be released from. Have you been locked down in your spirit? If so, just like I am praying for my kids to leave with enthusiasm to live life to its fullest. I believe we need to do the same. It is nothing like being a prisoner in your own mind!

I love Jeremiah 29:11 (NRSV), *I know the plans I have for you, says the Lord, plans for your welfare and not for harm, to give you a future with hope.*

Our age doesn't matter. Our looks don't matter. Our circumstances don't matter. For every individual, every life, God has a plan for the future. Even if you are reading this post from a hospital bed from which you never expect to leave, God has given you a future. Don't drop out of life for any reason. With Him, OUR BEST DAYS ARE YET TO COME, better than we can THINK or IMAGINE! So release yourself and KEEP IT MOVING!!

Model Goodness!

JOURNAL

_____

_____

_____

_____

_____

_____

_____

_____

_____

_____

_____

_____

_____

_____

_____

_____

_____

_____

_____

_____

_____

_____

Day 95
Journey ~ Is it LOVE In the Air?

Is it love in the air or just wishful thinking? If you know me I have no problem being transparent. Sometimes that can be bad but most times it is truly a blessing. So, with that said, for the last five months I have walked through something that truly rocked my world. It made me question everything I thought I knew. On the love day, I will stand before a judge who will bring down the gavel and say, "Your divorce is final." Wow! Since we are on the eve of the biggest celebrated LOVE DAY in our lives; I wanted to say whether you are in love, want to be in love, was in love and glad or sad it's over there is one love you will never have to question and that is the LOVE OF GOD!

Psalm 103:15-18 says, *"As for man, his days are like grass; he flourishes like a flower of the field; for the wind passes over it, and it is gone, and its place knows it no more. But the steadfast love of the Lord is from everlasting to everlasting."*

God loves us! It's not complicated or conditional, it's just a fact! Our human understanding can't comprehend the reason why, only that it's true. As much as we might want to explain it, dissect it, reason it out, we just can't. So, instead of wrapping ourselves in questions, wrap ourselves in HIS LOVE. HE HAS GIVEN US the very BEST HE HAS TO OFFER!

Model Goodness!

202

JOURNAL

_____
_____
_____
_____
_____
_____
_____
_____
_____
_____
_____
_____
_____
_____
_____
_____
_____
_____
_____
_____

Day 96
Journey ~ Good and Bad!

I can remember my mother saying to me many times as child, "Renee' you have to learn to take the good with the bad."

At the time I really didn't get it, but today I realize that both are just a part of life. I think during my youth something inside of me thought I could have a good day everyday and that is exactly what I strove for, only to face the saying my Mom reminded me of. Well, I am faced with this saying today, but what I know for sure is, My God IS ABLE!

In Ecclesiastes 7:14 it says, *When times are good, be happy; but when times are bad, consider: God has made the one as well as the other.*

We tend to think of God gratefully in the good times and ask for His help in the bad, but sometimes you have to consider that God brings good out of both. No matter what our feelings tell us, we can trust Him to work out His purpose in us at all times. He isn't bound by our feelings; He is bound by His Word. We should not be bound by our feelings either but by His PROMISES! I dare you to walk in PROMISE!

Model Goodness!

JOURNAL

_____
_____
_____
_____
_____
_____
_____
_____
_____
_____
_____
_____
_____
_____
_____
_____
_____
_____
_____
_____
_____
_____
_____
_____
_____

Day 97

Journey ~ Get Yo Umbrella!

Many things happen in our lives. Some of them are flukes and seem to come out of the blue. All the events work into a pattern helping to create us, create our path thru life, create our destiny. Sometimes we're influenced greatly by a traumatic storm, other times we are affected by what seems to be chance occurrences that change the entire pattern and course of our lives. We don't have to understand everything. Maybe we aren't supposed to. We don't have to be prepared for all the storms.

Sometimes the greatest learning occurs when we're caught off guard! Weather the storms, let them pass; keep your balance as best you're able. Remember to be flexible and sway with the winds like the tall trees in the forest. Let DESTINY have its way with YOU. GOD HAS IT ALL PLANNED OUT!

Model Goodness!

JOURNAL

_____
_____
_____
_____
_____
_____
_____
_____
_____
_____
_____
_____
_____
_____
_____
_____
_____
_____
_____
_____
_____
_____

Day 98
Journey ~ Lessons Learned

There is an old lesson, but it bears repeating and remembering. We don't have to let anyone control our lives, our choices, and our joy. Sometimes, no matter how much you love others it's time to let go and allow them walk their own path. Time to realize that it is your responsibility to walk your own. Go in love, Go in peace. Go in gentle power. You are responsible for your life. You are responsible for your choices. It doesn't matter what the other person does. You are still responsible for YOU. Take care of yourself, and then take it one step further. Love, nurture, honor, and respect YOURSELF! Only you can decide what you're going to do! But whatever you do remember to always.

Model Goodness!

JOURNAL

Day 99
Journey ~ Acceptance!

Acceptance is a powerful word, for it implies a willingness to listen and be open. Acceptance does not necessarily mean that I adopt another's point of view; it means I accept the right of another to have views different from my own. I accept people of different faiths, cultures and lifestyles. Each person is a child of God –divinely created and guided. I accept myself as well. I do not harshly judge my past mistakes or perceived shortcomings. I give myself the freedom to make mistakes, to have a unique point of view and to continue to learn and grow as a spiritual being.

By accepting myself and others, I embrace differences and celebrate the uniqueness of every individual. We were created on purpose. IT IS WHAT IS!

Model Goodness!

JOURNAL

_____

_____

_____

_____

_____

_____

_____

_____

_____

_____

_____

_____

_____

_____

_____

_____

_____

_____

_____

_____

_____

_____

_____

_____

_____

_____

Day 100
Journey ~ Being Present Fully!

Presence is a gift! Staying fully present for friends, family, and our lives. Staying in the moment, with our hearts open will change other people's lives and ours. Often we've learned out of habit or fear to be only partially present for ourselves, others, and our lives. We aren't certain what we feel our attention and energy are diverted to the next place, the next person. We're there…kind of!

There's another way, a better way. We take the risk of being vulnerable enough to share who we really are and to allow others to do the same. We become fully present for each moment and each person on our journey! Learn to release all that stands in the way of you and the present moment. Learn to let go of all that blocks you from being fully present for you and others. GIVE THE GIFT OF PRESENCE TO YOURSELF God is in this moment don't miss it!

In the television show, "Hawthorne," Jada Pickett Smith as (Nurse Hawthorne) was asked, what was she going to do about her situation? She answered, "I am going to show up for me."

Powerful! I am showing up for me today, for in doing so others will be blessed as well!

Model Goodness!

JOURNAL

_____
_____
_____
_____
_____
_____
_____
_____
_____
_____
_____
_____
_____
_____
_____
_____
_____
_____
_____
_____
_____
_____
_____

ABOUT THE AUTHOR

Esther Renee' Wright is a woman who is after God's heart and, is always on a mission to spread God's word. She is a teacher of the gospel, a chemical dependency counselor who absolutely loves assisting others with life issues.

She is the founder of Titus Works, Ministries, a vision she believes was downloaded specifically to her from God. This ministry has been created to spread the word freely to God's people. Titus based on the Word of God in Titus chapter 2, teaches us that the old shall be there to guide the young into a better life with Christ. This ministry strives to do this in a unique way. That through telephone empowerment conference calls, Esther Renee' with powerful speakers and topics is keeping it real with people and God.

Esther Renee', has been blessed to counsel, motivate, inspire and encourage others that they too can be a living testimony. She is a humble servant that exemplifies an attitude of gratitude. She will tell you, "I AM GRATEFUL FOR EVERYTHING."

With all of that said the most important thing she would like for you to know about her is that she loves God with all of her heart and wants nothing more than for God to be pleased with everything she does.

www.ingramcontent.com/pod-product-compliance
Lightning Source LLC
LaVergne TN
LVHW051048080426
835508LV00019B/1774